GW00454980

ECHOES OF HISTORY

Further details of Poppyland Publishing titles can be found at
www.poppyland.co.uk
where clicking on the 'Support and Resources' button
will lead to pages specially compiled to support this book
Join us for more Norfolk and Suffolk stories and background at
www.facebook.com/poppylandpublishing
and follow **@poppylandpub**

Echoes of History
Poppyland 1883–1914
by
David Thornton

To my parents, John and Iva Thornton, who loved Poppyland.

POPPYLAND
PUBLISHING

Copyright © 2017 David Thornton
First published 2017 by Poppyland Publishing, Cromer, NR27 9AN
www.poppyland.co.uk
ISBN 978-1-909796-34-8
All rights reserved. No part of this publication may be reproduced, stored in a retrieval system
  or transmitted by any means, mechanical, photocopying, recording or otherwise, without the
  written permission of the publishers.
Designed and typeset in 12 on 14.4 pt Gilgamesh
Printed by Lightning Source

Picture credits:

Eddie Anderson 25, 26
Author's Collection 16, 45, 57, 63, 66, 76, 103, 108,116, 120, 125, 150,158, 182
Cromer Museum 90 (CR09181), 99,113, 189 (CR0896), 190
Ron Fiske Collection 28, 29, 35, 38
Mr & Mrs Goffin 49
Richard Harbord 86
Geoffrey Kidd Collection 41, 107, 145, 165, 180, 194 (top)
Derek Paul 70, 74
Poppyland Collection 40, 78, 79, 81, 94, 120, 139, 148, 156, 157, 162, 167, 194 (bottom), 199
Poppyland Publishing 48, 177
Randall-Salter Magic Lantern Slide 105, 147, 191

Publisher's Note

The sources used for this book sometimes vary in their style. For instance, Scott's original
books used the term Poppy-Land, where style in recent years has been to say Poppyland.
Some Locker-Lampson correspondence hyphenates the name, some does not. We have
generally tried to follow the style in the appropriate quotation.

Associated titles from Poppyland Publishing:

Books

Poppyland in Pictures, Elizabeth Jones
Poppyland — Strands of Norfolk History, Peter Stibbons and David Cleveland
A Dictionary of Cromer and Overstrand History, Christopher Pipe
Cromer — Chronicle of a Watering Place, Martin Warren

DVDs

Poppyland - a documentary about Clement Scott
Overstrand - Our Village
Overstrand - Tide and Time

Contents

Acknowledgements

In the course of writing this book, I have been greatly assisted by a number of public bodies and individuals who have shown me the utmost courtesy and generosity in supplying information and illustrations without whose co-operation it would have been impossible to complete this book.

Among the former I wish to express my sincere thanks to the staff of Cromer Public Library for their unfailing help and courtesy; Alistair Murphy, Curator of the Cromer Museum for allowing me ready access to the extensive collection of local history material held at the Museum; the staff of the Norfolk Record Office at County Hall, Norwich and permission to publish references to the Gunton archives; the volunteers of the Norfolk Family History Society in St. Giles Street, Norwich; Barry Jennings, Honorary Sales Officer of the Great Eastern Railway Society Sales Emporium, for providing valuable information on G.E.R. rail services to Cromer and a copy of the article on Miller Jermy; to Justin Cavernelis-Frost, Archivist of the Rothschild Archive, London, for information in their collection; Gemma Pulton, archivist of the University of Exeter, for her help and advice in connection with the collection of du Maurier records held in their collection; the Chichester Partnership for permission to publish Isabel Scott's letter to her sister-in-law. Further afield, I thank the staff of Rochester University, New York State for making available the correspondence of Clement Scott held in their collection.

Many individuals have been helpful and encouraging. First and foremost I wish to thank Professor Leonée Ormond, Emerita Professor of Victorian Studies at Kings College, London, and author of the biography of Clement Scott's brother-in-law, George du Maurier, for her ready response to my initial request for advice, and subsequent interest, but above all for bringing her unrivalled knowledge of the period to bear in writing the Foreword.

I sincerely thank the following individuals: Eddie Anderson for kindly sharing with me his large archive collection on local families, and especially the Hoare family, for providing the two unpublished drawings of Samuel Hoare II and Cliff House; my sister, Mrs. Angela Bridge, for greatly assisting me in the research and together with her daughter-in-law, Mrs. Carol Bridge of Toronto, Canada, for driving to Rochester University, U.S.A., and perusing the collection of Clement Scott's letters in their collection; Charles Buxton for allowing me access to the Battersea archives at the Pleasaunce, Overstrand; Ms. Mari Chalk, a Steward at Felbrigg Hall, with whom I have consulted throughout the writing of this book and who offered advice and who critically read each chapter as it was completed; Peter Cox for allowing me to quote from his books on Sheringham; Peter and Janet Ellis for information on the Admiralty yacht, *Enchantress*; Richard Harbord, the architect and local historian, for providing invaluable information on the third and fifth Barons Suffield and for providing photographs of Gunton Hall; Geoffrey Kidd for his encouragement, advice and, as a member of a long-standing local family, for unselfishly sharing with me his unrivalled local knowledge and collection of photographs and documents on the area; Mrs. Irene Knockels for allowing me to see the fine collection of photographs, post cards and memorabilia built up by her late husband; Catherine McNulty for reading sample chapters from a younger reader's perspective; the author Angela Padmore for invaluable help with the Aesthetic Movemement.

I thank my wife, Marigold, for the patience and forbearance she showed in sharing her home so long with intruders such as Clement Scott, Isabel du Maurier, Louie Jermy, Lord and Lady Battersea, Oscar Wilde, Lillie Langtry and a host of others.

I begin the Introduction with a reference to those who are so captivated by the of charm Poppyland that on retirement they move into the area. One such couple who did just this are John and Barbara Mason who moved here on retirement from Kent. I first met Barbara while she was walking her beloved collie, Daisy, on the beach between Overstrand and Cromer a few years ago. It was Barbara's infectious love of Poppyland that first aroused my interest in its history, without which this book would not have been written. I thank her for the inspiration she afforded me.

Cromer parish church from the gardens of Garden Street, circa 1860.

Foreword

Poppyland, as David Thornton demonstrates, was an extraordinary late nineteenth century phenomenon. This region on the north coast of Norfolk takes its name from the poppies which grew in the cornfields, and from the title of a book, *Poppy-Land*, published in 1886 by the journalist, dramatic critic and poet, Clement Scott. Scott tells of his discovery of an unspoilt rural world, inhabited by fishermen and farmers. Dispatched to Norfolk to write articles for the *Daily Telegraph* (later incorporated into his book) in August 1883, he visited Cromer, already a seaside resort, although by no means the crowded and popular place it later became. Scott characterises Cromer as a place where people swam from bathing machines *and kept to a strict timetable going onto the beach in the morning, then onto the cliff in order to walk in one direction in the afternoon and in the opposite direction at sunset. The evening and night found them on the jetty.*

Unable to find accommodation in the town, Scott walked out along the cliffs and fields, through the nearby village of Overstrand and found a room in the Mill House, in the nearby hamlet of Sidestrand. This was the home of a miller with a taste for literature, Alfred Jermy, and his daughter Louie, to whose beneficial effect on their visitors a chapter of the book is dedicated. Close to Sidestrand Scott particularly noticed the ruined church tower, left standing as a guide for sailors after the falling cliff necessitated the movement of the church itself inland. The surrounding graveyard was the 'Garden of Sleep', the scene of one of Scott's poems, made famous as a popular song in a setting by Isidore de Lara.

Scott's friends advised him to travel to the Black Forest or the Alps, and he wondered why they could not enjoy Norfolk 'villages, old churches, dreamy farms, flowered lanes, woods and miles of heathland that are as empty and untenanted as if they were far removed from the confines of civilisation'. He expressed this bafflement, not only in *Poppy-Land*, but also in his poetry:

> I cannot confess to an envious minute,
> Since first this village I came across
> For the sea-sick traveller can't be in it
> With the usual gambol of pitch-and-toss!
> I wouldn't exchange your Pontresinas,
> Your Alpine valleys, and castled Rhine,
> For my morning 'weed' from a box of 'Finas,'
> And drink of cup of air like wine.
> The cosiest corner for holiday whiffs
> Is found in a hollow of Cromer cliffs!

(Lays and Lyrics, 1888)

There is a certain irony in the fact that Scott's enthusiasm for the place, and the publication of his book, by encouraging many to follow his example, undermined the peaceful setting. The coming of the railways to Cromer, in 1877 and 1887, for which there was now a demand, and the opening of hotels in the area all contributed to the creation of a different world. Before long facilities for golf at Cromer and cricket at Overstrand were introduced.

One thing which David Thornton's study makes very clear is the extent to which the early holiday makers and second home owners in Poppyland came from the highest class. The original landowners were often descendants of families associated with non-conformity and with opposition to slavery and several of the newcomers carried on this liberal tradition. Politicians, including three serving prime ministers and a later prime minister, Winston Churchill, together with actors and writers, came to Cromer and Overstrand to visit friends, or to take a break from busy lives, and some then acquired property or established a regular practice of visiting the area. One of the largest local landowners, Lord Suffield of Gunton Park, sold much of the land on which country houses and smaller properties were built. Suffield was a friend of Edward VII, who wanted to buy Gunton but had to be satisfied with Sandringham. Another visitor was Queen Victoria's artist daughter, Princess Louise, who stayed with Lord and Lady Battersea at their home, the Pleasaunce. The Batterseas' architect was Sir Edwin Lutyens who designed Overstrand Hall for the banker, Lord Hillingdon. Overstrand, a quiet rural scene when Scott first discovered it, came to be known as 'the millionaires' village'. The Batterseas, Cyril Flower and the former Constance de Rothschild, were among the grandest and most influential inhabitants. The great lawyer of the age, Sir George Lewis, bought the Danish Pavilion from the Paris exhibition and re-erected it as a holiday home in the same village. One surprising visitor who stayed in a hotel rather than a mansion was the Empress Elizabeth of Austria who (with good reason as she was later assassinated) insisted her staff oversee the baking of her bread in a local bakery.

Writers often came to escape the pace of London life, and to work in quieter surroundings. Remembering Scott's account of the strict etiquette for bathing in Cromer, it is amusing to learn that in September 1883, the poet Algernon Swinburne also turned his back on the resort beaches to stay at the Mill House in Sidestrand where he could swim 'in puris naturalibus'. Swinburne came to Norfolk with his great friend Walter Theodore Watts Dunton. In a letter to Watts Dunton's nephew, Herbert Mason, Swinburne explained that they were going to move from Cromer and that the Mill House had: 'a very pretty garden ¹[and] we think we shall be more comfortable & snug than in a hotel. It is not close to the sea like this, but quite near enough to go down and bathe whenever we like'. Swinburne was a lover of both cliff sand poppies, which he associated with Prosperine, and refers to both in several of his poems. Clement Scott's writing had encouraged him to come, and it is not hard to understand his attraction to this stretch of coast.

Oscar Wilde stayed in nearby village Felbrigg with his wife in 1892, when he was writing A Woman of No Importance and playing golf. David Thornton records a possible link with The Hound of the Baskervilles. George Meredith stayed at the Pleasaunce in 1896 and 1897 and E.F. Benson wrote of what is clearly the same mansion in his novel Limitations of 1896.

Among the visiting actors and actresses were Lillie Langtry, Ellen Terry, Edna May and Edward Compton. David Thornton also notes that four of the actresses who visited Poppyland were the subjects of proposals from aristocrats, with varying results.

Not surprisingly perhaps, one of the names which recurs in this book is that of the local doctor, Herbert Dent, who arrived in Cromer in 1889 and who published his memories of working with local families and their visitors. Quotations from Dent's *Reminiscences of a Cromer Doctor* have an immediacy which is remarkable as you encounter David Thornton's subjects in their everyday life, glimpsing their appearance, their clothes, their houses, and even their cars, in which Dr. Dent was given a lift. Dent told the story of the eleven-year-old Winston Churchill throwing an ink pot at the lady looking after him.

This privileged and enlivening lifestyle came to an abrupt end with the coming of war in 1914, the concluding year of this study. David Thornton clearly indicates that the first world war resulted in a complete change in Poppyland, that nothing was ever the same again. At least one of the great houses, Sea Marge, once the home of the financier Sir Edgar Speyer is now a hotel. In his introduction, David Thornton, hopes that he will be able to 'preserve' the history of Poppyland 'for future generations who may find it increasingly difficult with the passing of time to unravel the past in which they are nevertheless interested'.

This is exactly what he has indeed achieved, and this fascinating book will bring an extraordinary world alive for his readers.

Leonée Ormond

1   *Uncollected Letters of Algernon Charles Swinburne*, ed. T.L. Meyers, 2005, ii, 351.

Introduction

'Poppyland' is a name with which to conjure: golden sands; blue skies; happy holiday makers; fields of red poppies; Edwardian opulence; cheerful fishermen; happy children; long solitary walks through beautiful countryside with a faithful dog; golden sunrises and sunsets over the sea. For some it inspires nostalgic memories of the past; for others it draws like a magnet in the present. Walking my dog on the beach between Overstrand and Cromer, I have met people from all over the country who feel compelled to make a yearly visit to the area, pulled by the gravitational force of its peace and quiet and beautiful beaches, as the immemorial ebb and flow of the tide is pulled by the moon. Not a small percentage would like to move into the area because of the hold it exerts over them. Some are lucky enough to do so, as others aspire to move further along the coast to enjoy the beauty of the north Norfolk marshes.

But of those wishing to come to Poppyland, while the name may be familiar to them, their knowledge of Poppyland may be literally no more than that — the knowledge of a name. The knowledge of Poppyland is receding into the past. One individual thought the name derived from the First World War. Some know the name of the journalist Clement Scott who first used the term; to others it meant nothing. There are still echoes of the past — *Echoes of History* — discernible: vestiges of Lord and Lady Battersea's celebrated garden in Overstrand can still be seen from the footpath that ran through the middle of it; names such as Newhaven Close and Danish House Gardens refer to long lost houses; ornamental brickwork in some houses in Cliff Avenue, Cromer, refers to famous residents and visitors who once lived or stayed there.

The term 'Garden of Sleep' was often applied to Victorian graveyards but it acquired a specific meaning when applied to Sidestrand and the graves around the old church tower.

The term 'Poppy-Land' was coined in 1883. In August 1914, shortly after the outbreak of the Great War, holiday makers began leaving Cromer in droves, to the alarm of the landladies. The local cinema broadcast an appeal to visitors to remain, reminding viewers that Mrs. Clementine Churchill and her family were staying in Overstrand. Shortly afterwards they returned to London. It marked the end of an era.

Across the stage of Poppyland, while still at the height of its fame, may be found the names of royalty and blue-blooded aristocracy, bankers and industrialists, prime ministers and potentates, philanthropists and social reformers, newspaper proprietors and journalists, lawyers and architects, inventors and engineers, actors and actresses, poets and writers, clerics and scholastics and many more. They constitute a rich tapestry of social history. These *exalted personages in the course of a few years established Cromer on a pedestal of fame and helped it attain a vogue occupied by no other town of similar size in the kingdom.*[1] It may be seen as a sign of its status that at least five celebrities who patronised the area were painted by the society portrait painter John Singer Sargent: Ellen Terry, Sir George and Lady Lewis, Arthur Balfour and Lady Speyer. There is a further charcoal likeness of Margot Asquith.

The events described in this book took place over a hundred years ago. There are no living witnesses to enliven the scene with personal memories. Those wishing to open a window on the past must do so through the written word. One of the most valuable sources of information is to be found in a small book entitled *The Reminiscences of a Cromer Doctor*. Dr. Herbert Dent M.B.E. went to India as an army doctor in 1885. His heart was so damaged by an attack of malarial and typhoid fever that he was given a short time to live and retired from the army with a small pension in 1888 with the rank of major. He was greatly disappointed as he held the post of Staff Surgeon to Sir George Greaves, general commanding the Meerut Division, and his prospects of promotion were good.

His health improved. In June, 1889, he came to Cromer as an assistant to Dr. Fenner, an old hospital fellow student. He lived with him until his marriage in 1895. Dr. Dent regarded it as a *great descent* from his army position to be an assistant doctor in a fishing village, as Cromer was in those days. However, any notions he might have had in the way of

The little village of Overstrand required only the smaller Christ Church as St Martin's deteriorated. The rapid growth of the village in the Poppyland era brought about the restoration of the older building.

self-importance were soon squashed. One dark night he was sent on a baby case to Trimingham, some six miles away. On arrival a window was thrown open from a dimly lit room above. Into the wet and darkness came a voice, 'Is that Dr. Fenner?' 'No,' I replied, 'I'm his assistant, and have come in his place.' 'Well, go yow hoome and seend yower maaster; we don't want no boys here.'

Dr. Dent was scrupulous in his writing not to cause offence:

> In writing reminiscences, particularly when the lapse of time after all is a modest one, I deem it to be a writer's first duty, and more especially when that writer is a medical man, to take the utmost precautions to hurt the feelings of none and to abuse no confidence, even at the expense of having to discard many a good story and humorous situation likely to tickle the palate of the public.[2]

Nevertheless, Dr. Dent clearly had the human touch and possessed a good insight into human nature. The reminiscences, *with special application to the many more notable among the visitors to the district with whom I have been brought into touch,* are full of delightful anecdotes that help to bring Poppyland to life.

Too often today Poppyland is seen as merely a name, two dimensionally, as it were, a separate entity from wider life as a whole. This is to underestimate the extent to which Poppyland permeated society. In 1891 The *Daily Telegraph* advertised a play by J.M. Barrie extolling the beauties of Poppyland, among other locations. At much the same time a race horse named Poppyland was competing at Kempton Park, Leicester and Northampton. Cromer was news to all parts of the kingdom. In August, 1898, the *Aberdeen Telegraph* reported the names of those holidaying in the town. [see Chapter 7] At a slightly later date the fame of Poppyland was used to advertise Abdullah cigarettes in the *Tatler.* The first two lines of advertising doggerel read:

> Wrapt in a day dream of delight I stand
> Close to the sleeping heart of Poppyland.

Many of the visitors who patronised Poppyland in its heyday were successful men and women of outstanding ability and fame, often at the top of their respective professions and whose names were household words. I have tried to place them three dimensionally into the broader context of the social, cultural and intellectual life of their day. It is only by so doing and realising the influence they exercised upon contemporary life that the modern reader can appreciate just what a unique, interesting social phenomenon Poppyland turned out to be. I have not attempted to name them all, or every celebrity who owned a second home in Poppyland, or every new hotel that opened. It would be tedious to do so. In the following pages I have selected for fuller consideration some of the more interesting lives who made their name in their field of life and who deserve to be remembered today.

The birth place of Poppyland was the village of Sidestrand. It was here that the *Daily Telegraph* journalist Clement Scott stayed at the Mill House with the miller, Alfred Jermy, in 1883. Here he discovered the tower of the former Sidestrand church standing alone and abandoned on the cliff top, surrounded by a mass of red poppies and the graves of former parishioners. His flowery description of the area, his unbounded admiration for the miller's daughter, Louie, and her ready welcome to visitors, brought it to the attention of a wider audience through his articles. Sidestrand was thus the epicentre of Poppyland. Because it was contiguous with Sidestrand, Overstrand from the start was considered to be part of Poppyland.

The author is well aware there is a strong body of local opinion today which considers Poppyland to be begin with the drinking trough commemorating Clement Scott just east of Cromer and ending with the boundary between Sidestrand and Trimingham. However, epicentres produce shock waves which travel distances and cannot be ignored. The water-colourist G. Parsons-Norman described the area between Sheringham and Mundesley and beyond in a book he called *Poppyland*, illustrating it with twelve of his own watercolours abounding in red poppies.[3] There is no date in the publication, but it must be prior to 1913, the year of his death. It includes many of the beauty spots that so captivated the early visitors to the area. Parsons-Norman recognised Sidestrand as the birth place of *Poppyland: To the tiny village of Sidestrand properly belongs the spot where all the accumulation of romance fostered in Poppyland is centred.* He considered this whole area to be part of Poppyland: *The way back to West Runton down Davy Hill, with the woods on the right and the Camp on the left, is not the smallest charm of this bit of Poppyland.* Of Mundesley he wrote: *Like all the rest of the coast claiming a share in Poppyland district, the cliffs are perhaps the greatest charm, not only for their grandeur and the fine view obtained, but for the pure, fresh healthy air.* A poster of slightly later date issued by the London and North Eastern Railway Company proclaims *Cromer, the Centre of Poppyland.*

The author firmly endorses the view that the centre of Poppyland is the villages of Sidestrand and Overstrand, but recognises the fact that those areas of natural beauty so loved by the early visitors to the area may legitimately be considered to be within the area affected by the shock waves emanating from this epicentre. This includes the cliffs of the north Norfolk coast from Mundesley to Sheringham and specific beauty spots a mile or so inland.

This book comes with what might be described as a 'health warning'. There is a darker side to Poppyland in more ways than one. Many of the principal characters who figure in the history of Poppyland were well known, wealthy and influential. It is inevitable they have attracted the greatest coverage. This must not be allowed to distort the overall historical picture of the harsh living conditions of the time, which often resulted in the poverty of less well paid working people who were to be found in the towns, villages and hamlets of Poppyland. While Lord Battersea was plying the shopkeepers of Battersea and Balham with his best champagne

Cromer, the 'Centre of Poppyland', in the words of the railway company. The beginning of the influx of visitors encouraged the lengthening of the promenades. About 1895, the jetty is still in place.

20 years after Scott's first visit, the railway was extended to provide a 'halt' for the golf course, Overstrand station as seen in this picture and a line through to Mundesley and thence to North Walsham.

at the annual cricket match between them and *the serfs of Overstrand* [4] in 1898 many were still drawing their drinking water from wells.

Two important written sources for information on Poppyland were journalist Clement Scott, and also Lady Constance Battersea in her *Reminiscences.*[5] Both were writing from privileged positions; both saw life from their own perspective; both presented at times an idealistic interpretation of their experiences. Clement Scott romanticises the work of agricultural labourers, particularly in relation to the harvest:

> *When I see these healthy labourers, their buxom wives, and strong-limbed children, I cannot find it in my utmost sympathy to pity these tillers of the soil, notwithstanding the fact of their twelve odd shillings a week wage and abated harvest money.*[6]

As Cromer was gaining in its reputation for being an exclusive watering resort for the middle and upper classes in the mid-nineteenth century, farm labourers worked a full six days a week *for a wage which varied from a trough of 6/6 a week in 1851 to a peak of 10/6 in the boom year of 1868.* Allowing for part time earnings by a wife and children the total weekly income may have reached 15/-.[7] By the time Scott was writing, conditions may have improved, but conditions were still hard and there was much poverty. It is small wonder the local newspapers record many instances of poachers being brought before the local magistrates and fined. On July 20th, 1906, the *Eastern Counties Agricultural Labourers & Small Holders Union* was established at a conference of agricultural workers at the Angel Hotel, North Walsham. In 1910 there were major strikes at Trunch and Knapton on the edge of Poppyland for an additional 1/- a week extra. In some instances to belong to a union meant instant dismissal. Wealthy visitors to Poppyland must have benefitted the local economy. It would form a useful topic for a Ph.D. thesis to determine just how this influx of wealth benefitted the poorest in Poppyland.

In her *Reminiscences* Lady Battersea refers to the poverty she encountered in Overstrand itself. She was, at times, generous and kind to individuals. But all is not always as it seems. In 1977 the author interviewed the late Harry Curtis who worked for some years as Lady Battersea's chauffeur. He spoke of the liveried servants. In his words *everything had to be just so. If you worked for the Battersea's, they owned you, body, mind and spirit.*

Even behind the story of the emergence of Poppyland itself there is a darker side. The popular version is that Clement Scott arrived one day at Cromer by train, walked along sunny deserted cliffs, found Sidestrand Mill house, asked for lodgings, was welcomed by the miller's daughter, Louie Jermy, fell in love with the area and invented Poppyland. This is true as far as it goes, but nevertheless it is a veneer, covering a deeper, all-together sadder course of events that will be seen below.

None of the above detracts in any way from the uniqueness of Poppyland. Poppyland does not depend on the reporting of Clement Scott seeing life through rosy-coloured spectacles, but rather on its own merits. It is an area of infinite beauty and peace, where sun and sand, sea and sky, woods and walks may be enjoyed to the full, where friendship is important.

1   H.C. Dent, *The Reminiscences of a Cromer Doctor: A record of many famous personages, amusing anecdotes and stories of diplomats, actors and others* (Holt: Norfolk Press Syndicate, 192-?).
2   Dent, p. 4.
3   G. Parsons-Norman, *Poppyland* (Norwich: Jarrold, 1894).
4   John Jolliffe, *Raymond Asquith: life and letters* (London: Collins, 1980).
5   Constance Battersea, *Reminiscences* (London: Macmillan, 1922).
6   Clement Scott, *Poppy-land*, 4th ed. (Norwich: Jarrold, 1895).
7   R.S. Joby, *The East Norfolk Railway* (Norwich: Klofron, 1975).

1

Historical Origins

Four factors over a long period of time contributed to the creation of Poppyland. The first of these was the rise in the popularity of sea bathing. This practice had been given a boost in 1789 when King George III, Queen Caroline and four of their daughters visited Weymouth. The King bathed in the sea, using a bathing machine. As he entered the water a band, secreted in a neighbouring machine, played the National Anthem. There was, however, a bathing machine in Cromer ten years previously in 1779.

In 1780 an advertisement under the heading *SEA BATHING* reminded the public that:

> The Season for Bathing being nearly at hand, the Proprietors of the Cromer Machine take this opportunity of returning Thanks to all those Gentlemen, Ladies and others, who so obligingly favoured them with their Companies last year, and at the same Time beg Leave to solicit their further Favours, as well as those of the Neighbourhood in general. Some additional Improvements having been made to it this Season, and no Expense spared for rendering it not only safe, but neat and commodious, it is hoped it may without Vanity claim a Preference to every other Bathing Machine. Proper and careful Persons will attend every Day as usual.[1]

In 1792 it was reported that *Cromer has for some years past been a summer resort of much genteel company, on account, as well of the beauty and pleasantness of the country about it as of the salubrity of the air and the convenience of the place for bathing.*

A further advertisement exists for the sale of *an exceeding good* dwelling-house in Cromer in 1798 which was well worth attention as a residence for sea-bathing, having been let as lodgings for some years.[3]

The rise in the popularity of Cromer for sea bathing was given impetus by William Windham III of Felbrigg Hall. As a War Minister in the Napoleonic conflict, he was a national celebrity of the first rank. He was widely read and a good conversationalist with a wide circle of friends. Although much of his time was spent in London, visitors to Felbrigg also visited Cromer. In July, 1790, Windham recorded in his diary:

> The evening of our going to Cromer was very fine, and the party all together very pleasant. We went, for the first time for me, to the 'New Inn,' which promises to be a great accession to our comfort.

By 1800 Cromer was sufficiently developed as watering place for a guide book of the area to be published. This was written by Edmund Bartell and was sold in London, Norwich and in Cromer by J. Rust.[4] It provides a snapshot into the embryonic state of the future holiday resort. His description is careful and judicial. The houses in general were indifferent and the rents very high, although tolerable accommodation is to be found for strangers, from one to three guineas a week. There were no places of public amusement, no rooms, balls, nor card assemblies. There was, however, a small circulating library, consisting chiefly of a few novels. It was regretted there was no large and well conducted inn for those who visited Cromer. The author speculated whether the summer trade would carry an inn keeper through the winter months, but thought it might be successful.

Various aspects of maritime life occupied the author's attention. He recorded the bathing machines were very commodious, and the bather a careful, attentive man.

> At Cromer the shore, also, which is a fine firm sand, not only renders the bathing agreeable, but when the tide retires, presents such a surface for many miles as cannot be exceeded. The sea too is one of those objects that appears to have the constant power of pleasing.

The fishing industry was of unfailing interest.

> The fishery, independent of the pleasure we receive from the consideration of the support it brings to a numerous, hardy, and in many instances, an industrious set of people, is not without effect in a picturesque point of view. The different preparations for the voyage; the groupes[sic] of

figures employed in different ways — some carrying a boat down to the water's edge, some carrying oars, nets, masts and sails; while others, in a greater state of forwardness are actually pulling through the breakers, form a scene of the most busy, various and pleasing kind.

Bartell thought that with the provision of a *large and well-conducted inn*, Cromer in a few years stood a *chance of rivaling[sic] some of the more celebrated bathing places for the number, as well as the consequence of its visitors.* His supposition proved to be right. Cromer quickly developed its reputation for gentility.

The company is seldom numerous, but not unfrequently of a more pleasing species than is found in other greater watering places. An adventurer, a fortune hunter, or a black-leg is never seen within its precincts.[5]

The full title of Edmund Bartell's book was *Observations Upon The Town of Cromer Considered as a Watering Place, and the Picturesque Scenery in Its Neighbourhood.* Much of it is devoted to a description of the surrounding countryside and its beauty. He transports the reader to places as far away as Mundesley in the east, to Holt and Sheringham in the west. He includes descriptions of such notable landmarks as Felbrigg Hall and its grounds, Thorp-Market church, North Repps Cottage, Blickling Hall, Wolterton and Upper Sheringham.

James Bartell was an amateur artist. He became a member of the Norwich Society in 1808, when he exhibited two views of Cromer in the exhibition.[6] It was possibly both his writing and his paintings that drew other artists to Cromer, thus helping to spread the knowledge and popularity of the area. John Crome, John Sell Cotman and Henry Ladbrooke all exhibited views of Cromer in 1809. Cotman married the daughter of a Felbrigg farmer in 1809.

The London artist William Collins visited the Norfolk coast in 1815 and stayed with the Norwich School painter James Stark. Stark took him to Cromer where he spent two months making studies of the local scenery. During this stay he painted a picture he entitled *Scene of the Coast of Norfolk*, which was purchased by the future King William IV when Prince Regent.

In a letter dated 8th September, 1803, to her married sister, Elizabeth Fry, Richenda Gurney described a typical day at Cromer.[7] Enjoying the seaside was clearly important:

I give thee an idea of how we are going on, I will tell thee how we generally pass the day. The weather since we came has on the whole been very fine, so imagine us before breakfast, without troutbecks (hats) on and coloured gowns, running in all directions on the sands, jetty &. After breakfast we receive callers from the other houses, and fix with them the plans for the day; after this we now and then get an hour's quiet for reading and writing. At eleven we go down in numbers to bathe and enjoy the sands, which about that time look beautiful: most of our party and the rest of Cromer company come down, and bring a number of different carriages, which have a very pretty effect. After bathing, we either ride on horseback or take some pleasant excursion or other. I never remember enjoying the sea so much, and never liked Cromer a quarter so well.

The day before yesterday we spent at Sherringham[sic], wandering about the woods, and sketching all morning. Every one met at a beautiful spot for dinner, with three knives and forks and two or three plates for twenty-six people. All manner of games took place after dinner. We completed our day by a delightful musical evening.

Thus, eighty years before Clement Scott arrived by train at Cromer and invented the term Poppyland, its unique characteristics were being revealed. It was an area renowned for its sea bathing and magnificent beaches and sand; it was an area of glorious scenery of woods, valleys, heaths and gorse ideal for picnics, walking and horse riding; it provided wonderful sun-rises and sun-sets over the sea; the area was enriched by the constant movement of the sea and not a little by the hard working community of fishermen who were a constant source of interest; it was a relief from the dirt, the rush and bustle of London life; it was an area that offered few of the entertainments to be enjoyed in sophisticated town life; because of its remoteness a well deserved aura of gentility and exclusiveness grew up round it.

From the earliest days of its rise as a sea-bathing centre, an inner circle of five families who became inter-related, had purchased larger houses in the area. Their descendants exerted a considerable influence on Cromer and the locality for much of the nineteenth century. These were the Hoare, Gurney, Barclay, Buxton and Birkbeck families. They originated from widely different areas, but they had much in common. They were engaged in business, principally cloth weaving, banking and brewing with a high moral tone.

Samuel Hoare (I) brought his family from Ireland in the mid-eighteenth century and settled in Stoke Newington. At the age of fourteen his son, Samuel Hoare (II), was apprenticed to Henry Gurney of Norwich to learn the trade of a cloth manufacturer. On completing his apprenticeship in 1772, he entered business and was made a partner in the Banking House of Bland and Barnett, of 62, Lombard Street.[8] The name of Hoare was added to the title. The firm traded under the sign of the Black Horse. The business went through further name changes. In 1864 the bank merged with Hanbury & Lloyd, also of Lombard Street. It

eventually merged into LLoyd's, who thus acquired the famous sign of the Black Horse, still in use today.

While in Norwich Samuel Hoare (II) became friendly with Henry's nephew, John Gurney. The two friends visited Cromer together. They found *the place furnished such poor accommodation that one of their beds was obliged to be lengthened with chairs before it could be slept in.*[9] On May 15th, 1776, Samuel Hoare (II) married Sarah Gurney, the elder daughter of John's uncle, the late Samuel Gurney of Keswick Hall. Sarah died on January 31st, 1783, shortly after giving birth to her fourth child and first son, Samuel, (III). Samuel II's daughter recalled,

John Gurney first came to Cromer with Samuel Hoare.

Samuel Hoare II and John's descendants intermarried and affected Cromer social life for a hundred years.

In the autumn of 1789 we first went to Cromer ; Our house in the churchyard did not abound in comforts; and we particularly needed them, from having caught the measles from one of our men- servants. My father had happily had the ill before, and nursed my mother and all of us with the greatest care and tenderness. He went about from room to room feeding us with peaches on a fork. He was delighted with Cromer. A zealous sportsman, he found abundance of amusement. And, though from having no land, there was some jealousy between him and those who had, the pleasure far out-balanced the pain.[10]

This was more serious than it might appear at first. At that time, *even a well-to-do landowner was quite content to live the greater part of the year on his estate, amusing himself with the sport which satisfied the moderate needs of those days.*[11] Thus in shooting on other land-owner's property Samuel Hoare (II) was violating an established way of life. In 1801 Samuel Hoare (II) purchased Cliff

Cliff House, Cromer, was purchased by Samue Hoare II in 1801 and owned by the Hoare famiy for the greater part of the 19th century.

House on the Overstrand road, as a shooting box and holiday home. In 1807 Samuel Hoare (II) purchased the manor of Sidistron-Poynings.[12] He continued to shoot until 1820 when poor health prevented it and he died in 1825.

Samuel Hoare's friend, John Gurney, was the second of the four children of John Gurney of Magdalen Street, Norwich, all of whom exercised considerable influence through their descendants in helping to create the conditions that eventually led to the creation of Poppyland. These four were Richard, John, Joseph and Rachel. Richard Gurney's younger sister, Rachel, was married to the brewer David Barclay of Bury Hill, near Dorking, who purchased North Repps Hall in 1790. Rachel died in 1794, aged 49. In 1795 David Barclay sold the Hall to his brother-in-law, Richard. Richard never lived there, using the land to pursue his favourite hobby of shooting. The Hall has remained in the possession of the Gurney family to this day.

In 1775 John Gurney married Catherine Bell of Tottenham. John Gurney was for many years a wool-stapler and spinner of worsted yarn. John and Catherine produced a family of twelve children, one of whom died young. The family moved to Earlham Hall, Norwich, in 1786. Catherine was a devoted and much loved mother. Many years later her daughter Hannah Buxton wrote:

We, the younger girls, were spending the morning at the farther end of the kitchen garden, old nurse with us. Becky came to say a baby was born, and I remember the party of children allowed to go in to see the baby, holding onto each other's frock in an orderly line. Not two years after, I remember them in a similar line walking past their dying mother.[13]

Mrs. Catherine Gurney died on 17th November, 1792, aged 38. Her eldest daughter, Catherine, became head of the Earlham household, responsible for nine younger children. Long afterwards she wrote:

Here then we were left, I not seventeen, at the head, wholly ignorant of common life, from the retirement in which we had been educated, quite unprepared for filling an important station, and unaccustomed to act on independent principle. Still, my father placed me nominally at the head of the family — and continual weight and pain which wore my health and spirits. I never again had the joy and glee of youth.

It is recorded that the two motherless Barclay and Gurney families joined forces for a holiday at North Repps when a combined number of twenty-two children used to stand in a row on the beach.[14]

Many of the children of John and Catherine Gurney of Earlham made their mark in public life or made marriages that considerably influenced the future character of the Cromer area. In 1806 Louisa Gurney married Samuel Hoare III. It was natural she would want to spend her honeymoon at Cliff House, the home of her father-in-law. Louisa died in 1836, aged 50. One of their sons, John Gurney Hoare, also known as Samuel IV, married Caroline Barclay from Bury Hill in 1837.

In 1809 Louisa's sister, Hannah, married Thomas Fowell Buxton, who was allied with Edward, 3rd Lord Suffield, of Gunton Park and Cromer, William Wilberforce and others, in abolishing slavery in the British Empire by Act of Parliament in 1833. Since the date of the wedding, Thomas had been in the habit of renting Cromer Hall for the season from the Wyndham family for the shooting. After the destruction of the Hall by fire in 1828 he rented North Repps Hall from Richard Gurney. It was his home for the rest of his life, although he owned Colne House, Cromer. His widow, the much loved and respected Lady Hannah Buxton, died there in 1872.

About this time Joseph Gurney, the brother of Richard, John and

Rachel above, purchased a house and estate a little way out of Cromer on the road to Overstrand as a holiday home and named it The Grove, after his house in Norwich. By 1809 his estate extended to twenty-nine acres. The estate was sold to Sir William Birkbeck in 1828. Joseph Gurney's daughter, Elizabeth, married Robert Barclay in 1814. About the time of the marriage Robert bought a house in Cromer known as The Cottage, situated between The Grove and Cliff House. It eventually became known as The Warren. Robert enlarged it, as did his son Joseph Gurney Barclay. It was demolished in 1975.

The influence of the Gurney family was further extended when in 1793 Bartlett Gurney[15] built North Repps Cottage. The 'cottage' was designed

The Warren, c.1860. Originally known as The Cottage, it was purchased by Robert Barclay and subsequently enlarged. It was demolished in 1975.

by William Wilkins in the Gothic style. The unusual style for the times was a matter of great interest and attracted sight-seers from Cromer for many years. It was originally known as The Hermitage. This was the cottage that so charmed Clement Scott on his drive from Cromer on the evening of his first night in Sidestrand. (see Chapter 2)

Within a short period of time other families with whom the Hoare and Gurney families were friendly had followed their example and either purchased houses or holiday homes in the area. North Lodge was built on the cliff top just east of Cromer. The original plan is dated 1838.[16]

In 1857 it became the summer residence of Joseph Hoare, eldest son of Samuel and Louisa Hoare of Cliff House. The above named families and others closely related to them, were largely on friendly terms. Children of subsequent generations were linked by the stronger ties of marriage. Religion also strengthened these ties. Some were practicing Quakers. Others belonged to the established Church, but many shared a fervent evangelical faith, which resulted in philanthropic good works, especially the abolition of slavery and prison reform. These families formed an homogeneous and influential whole which helped to preserve the

North Lodge, Cromer, c.1870. John Gurney Hoare, also known as Samuel IV, owner of Cliff House, middle row right; his wife Caroline (née Barclay) on his left; his eldest son, Joseph, owner of North Lodge, to left: Lady Parry, centre; other members of the family.

exclusivity of the neighbourhood for many years.

However, not everyone was happy with the coming of the Hoare family into the neighbourhood. In a letter dated 29th November, 1820, written from Brussels, Vice Admiral William Lukin[17] wrote to the Reverend Cremer Cremer of Beeston Hall:[18]

My natural object as having an eventual stake in the neighbourhood, is to keep all my old neighbours together. I really, my dear Cremer, want no man's land; but what I want, though I should not like publicly to hold to that language, is to keep all men as Hoare away if possible, and there is no reasonable sacrifice that I would not make to effect that object.

I like and have always liked what may be termed I hope without arrogance native consequency, and I am always tenacious of its invasion and hence my dislike of Cromer. There is certainly in the human mind a natural desire to level everybody above us to our own standard, coupled as it always is with a proportionate desire of not lowering ourselves or of elevating others up to us; and it is from this natural propensity of our minds that I dislike such men as Hoare and others, under the mask of a watering-place among us.

Vice Admiral Lukin clearly regarded Samuel Hoare as an upstart. But equally he may have been referring to the custom currently prevailing that when visiting spas or watering-places social barriers were broken down. The aristocracy, who at other times would not have mixed with even genteel society, mixed freely in these places. This was certainly the case in Cromer:

There is nothing here of that mutual suspicion which leads strangers to keep each other at a distance: even our natural reserve appears to be laid aside; a stranger no sooner arrives than he is adopted into all the parties of the of the town.

Vice Admiral Lukin was not successful in preventing the Hoare family from becoming established in Cromer. Indeed, both his descendants and those of the Admiral played a significant role in the life of the local community into the Poppyland era itself. Samuel Hoare's (II) great grandson, Samuel Hoare (V), 1841–1915, was elected Member of Parliament for Norwich in a by-election in 1886, holding the seat until 1906 when he stood down. He was created a baronet in 1899. His son, Samuel Hoare (VI), 1880–1959, was for many years a leading Conservative politician. For much of the 1920s he served as Minister of State for Air. He was Foreign Secretary in 1935, Home Secretary, 1937–39 and Ambassador to Spain 1940-44. He was created the first Baron Templewood in 1942.

Vice Admiral Lukin had a family of six sons and six daughters two of whose daughters in future years were to play a significant role in the history of Poppyland. (see Chapters 6 and 12).

As the century wore on, the population of Cromer gradually increased and the size of the inter-related families grew. The population of 676 in 1801 had risen to 1232 in 1841. It was recorded at this time that:

> Cromer now contains many comfortable private lodging-houses, as well as apartments for the accommodation of visitors, as also some respectable inns. A number of houses called The Crescent, have been built within the last ten years, and are a great acquisition.[19]

However,

> The rent of houses is high, and consequently, that of lodgings is the same: the latter may be had at the rate of from one guinea and a half to three guineas and a half: entire houses from four to six guineas a week: those of the latter price, of which there are not more than four or five, make up ten beds, and are therefore capable of accommodating a large family.

The exclusivity and gentility of Cromer became more pronounced:

> During the season, a person, who is paid gratuitously, acts as a keeper of the jetty, whose business it is to prevent improper persons from obtruding themselves, and to preserve good order. We know not whether he has the power to forbid the smoking of cigars, but we certainly think that such ought to be the case; and we would add, that we can hardly believe that any real gentleman would require an admonition on such a point. Servants in livery and all common persons are not allowed at this time.

Common persons were, however, allowed on the jetty on Sundays. The reference above to the desirability of banning smoking of cigars on Cromer jetty is better understood by some comments Lady Nevill made on smoking:

> Smoking-rooms in country houses were absolutely unknown, and such gentlemen as wished to smoke after the ladies had gone to bed used, as a matter of course, to go either to the servants' hall or to the harness-room in the stables, where at night some sort of rough preparation was generally made for their accommodation. To smoke in Hyde Park,

even up to comparatively recent years, was looked upon as absolutely
unpardonable, while smoking anywhere with a lady would have been
classed as an almost disgraceful social crime.[20]

In 1864 Ellen Buxton recorded in her diary on her arrival at North
Repps Hall: *there was a good party when we arrived there. We were so full we*
had not a bed to spare, we were (with all the servants) fifty-six in the house
… so there was no lack of family.[21]

Later in the century Louise Hoare recalled that in the autumn her
parents, grand-parents, first, second and third cousins all congregated
in Cromer for a combined family holiday.

The third influential factor in the creation of the nature of Poppyland,
was lack of adequate public transport. This difficulty was succinctly
summed up in Jane Austen's *Emma:*

> *If Mr. Perry can tell me how to convey wife and five children a distance of*
> *one hundred and thirty miles with no greater expense or inconvenience*
> *than a distance of forty I shall be as willing to prefer Cromer to South*
> *End as he would.*

The first section of the Norwich—Cromer Turnpike road to Aylsham
was opened in 1794. Many of the subscribers were local land owners
or farmers hoping to find an quicker way of getting their produce
to market. The Aylsham—Cromer section followed in 1811, with an
extension to the Spread Eagle, Erpingham. This was no doubt for the
benefit of Lord Walpole at Wolterton Hall. It is interesting to note that
one of the subscribers to the Cromer extension was George Cooke
Turner, Inn Keeper of Cromer, who subscribed £100.[22] Good roads were
in the interest of his inn and of the holiday business. The road ran from
the entrance of the city of Norwich where St Augustine's Gate formerly
stood to the first house at the entrance of the town of Cromer where the
road joins the road from Overstrand.

The turnpike trustees were given considerable powers to keep the
roads under their jurisdiction free from obstruction to ensure the safe
passage of travellers. All boundaries in the rural areas had to be secure
against the incursion of farm animals, especially pigs.

In 1854 two coaches left Cromer daily at 8 a.m. for Norwich to connect
with the London train. *The Ocean* departed from Tucker's Hotel and *The*
Star from The Bell Vue. With variations between summer and winter

timetables this schedule continued until the coming of the railway. Travelling was far from comfortable:

> Sir, Being desirous last Saturday of visiting Cromer, I determined to brave the inclemency of the weather and the inconvenience of the road. Arriving at the Royal Hotel I beheld numerous blank faces gazing upwards at the mountainous aspect of the piled luggage. There were twenty-three passengers beside a supernumerary and the coachman. We take our places. Conceive, sir, our horror when we discover that our destinies are entrusted to a stout individual who has not omitted to taste the glass, which inebriates as well as cheers. We start, and proceed at a sharp trot through the city, more than once striking the kerb, and once the gable of a house, which dislocates the luggage, and almost knocks off a passenger. From St. Faith's to Aylsham , in spite of wind, rain, and all remonstrances, our horses are driven up-hill and down-hill at full speed. The Aylsham coach a-head possesses some all powerful attraction. Safe to Aylsham at all events. Our coachman disappears for a time at Aylsham and Roughton probably to dry his wet clothes, but with such beneficial effect upon his nerve that he dashes our swaying and top-heavy vehicle down Cromer-hill at a full gallop without the needless incumbrance of a drag. Well, sir, we arrived ducked, but safe; but no second adventure, under similar circumstances will be attempted by,

> Your obedient servant,

> POOR OUTSIDE.[23]

The date and stile of driving strongly suggests the coachman was William Frederick Windham, known locally as 'Mad Windham'.

In addition to coaches, an omnibus ran for the use of families, but this was a slow and uncomfortable mode of transport. Carriers' carts travelled between local market towns. When the railway arrived in Norwich, residents of Cromer wanting to catch the morning train to London had to catch Blythe's carrier's cart to Norwich, where they put up overnight. With the penetration of railways into rural areas, Turnpike Trusts gradually became obsolescent and were wound up. With the imminent arrival of the railway into Cromer in 1877, the clerk of the Norwich—Cromer Turnpike Trust received a letter from the Local

Government Board concerning the *discontinuance of the Trust which pointed out what was necessary to be done.* The last meeting was held in 1877.

The fourth important factor in the fashioning of Poppyland was the late arrival of the railways into Cromer. 1848 saw the opening of a railway line from Norwich to Yarmouth which quickly became the resort of the rail-borne masses, while Cromer, equidistant from Norwich, was confirmed as an alternative watering-place for the rich who wanted a quiet rest. Some years later Clement Scott recorded the difference between Yarmouth and Cromer.

> *The children at Cromer, so far as I have observed, are all good children. There are few babies and bottles. The sands are not turned into a nursery. Thus far I have not seen a perambulator or a goat-chaise.*

> *At Yarmouth babies swarm between one jetty and the other. Holes and hollows are dug in the sands, and down into it the miserable infant is plunged, with a feeding-bottle in its mouth, whilst the nursemaid turns aside and flirts with the photographer's assistant. Rations are served out at Yarmouth by the head nurse, seemingly most appetising to the hungry family, although they consist of sanded bread-and-butter or scraps of bread and cheese produced from a reticule.*

Until the arrival of the railway in Cromer private coaches, together with horses, had to travel by rail to Norwich on carriage trucks and were then driven to their destination. As a type, carriage trucks went back to the very beginnings of the Eastern Counties Railway, a small number being available on its opening day in 1839 for the conveyance of private horse drawn road carriages. They provided an ideal means of travel, much faster and more comfortable than by road, the occupants travelling in first class security and seclusion.

In September, 1864, the large family of Thomas Fowell Buxton travelled from their home in Leytonstone to spend a holiday with their Gurney relations at North Repps Hall. Ellen Buxton records the journey to North Repps in her diary.[24] A sense of excitement and adventure pervades the description: *Oh, such a delicious journey we had!* she wrote. A total of eight horses were loaded into the train at Stratford, together with the carriage:

A large gathering of the Buxton family – inset is Northrepps Hall in the 19th century.

Soon the train came up and it was the greatest interest to us all getting into the saloon carriage. It certainly was most comfortable and beautifully fitted up. There was a table in the middle, two nice easy chairs, a sofa fixed to the wall at one side. There was also a little carriage opening out of this big one, which we called the nursery, and there was a wash hand basin, and a place for the luggage. At about 12 o'clock we spread out our beautiful luncheon on the table, and were a long time eating it.

On arrival at Norwich they watched the horses being taken out of their boxes: little Derry looked perfectly self-possessed as though nothing surprised him. However, the journey was far from over and still held some surprises, principally because of Derry. Now Derry was excessively naughty, if we tried to hunt him one way, he was sure to turn down the wrong road on purpose. Eventually he became so unbearably wicked that he had to be ridden home without stirrups or bridle by another of the party. Ellen Buxton commented: I have not put down one half of all the wicked deeds that Derry did, he was just like a pig but so clever and looked so pleased with his own cleverness.

The railway eventually reached Cromer in 1877. (see Chapter 6)

However, by 1883 revenue from passenger traffic into Cromer station was still poor. At the end of August that year *The Daily Telegraph* sent its reporter, Clement Scott, with the authority of the Great Eastern Railway Directors, to write up the area for the newspaper.

1   *Norfolk Chronicle*, 27th May, 1780.
2   *The Universal British Directory*, London, 1793–1798.
3   *Norfolk Chronicle*, 14th April, 1798.
4   Edmund Bartell Jnr., *Observations upon the Town of Cromer Considered as a Watering Place* (Holt, 1800), p. 50.
5   *Monthly Register and Encyclopaedic Magazine*, 1800.
6   Andrew Hemingway, *The Norwich School of Painters, 1803–1833* (Oxford: Phaidon, 1979), p. 29.
7   Augustus J. Hare, *The Gurneys of Earlham* (London: George Allen, 1895), vol. 1, p. 128.
8   Samuel Hoare's mother was Grizel Gurnell. She was the daughter of Jonathan Gurnell, a banker.
9   Sarah Hoare and Hannah Hoare, *Memoirs of Samuel Hoare* (London: Headley Brothers, 1911), p. 20.
10   Hoare, p. 20.
11   Ralph Nevill, *The Life & Letters of Lady Dorothy Nevill* (London: Methuen, 1919), pp. 47–48.
12   Christobel Hoare (Mrs. Ivo Hood), The History of an East Anglian Soke: *studies in original documents* (Bedford: Time Publishing Co., 1918).
13   Hare, p. 20.
14   Walter Rye, *Cromer Past and Present* (Norwich: Jarrold, 1889), p. 145
15   Bartlett Gurney was the son of Henry Gurney to whom Samuel Hoare II had been apprenticed.
16   Christopher Pipe, *A Dictionary of Cromer and Overstrand History* (Cromer: Poppyland Publishing, 2010), p. 145.
17   William Windham III, d. 1810, was the last of his line. He bequeathed Felbrigg to his widow for life, then to the grandson of his mother by her first marriage, William Lukin. The latter had to wait to 1824 to enter into his inheritance, when he changed his name to Windham. He died in 1833.
18   R.W. Ketton-Cremer, *Felbrigg: the story of a house* (London: Rupert Hart-Davis, 1962), p. 229.
19   Bartell.
20   Ralph Nevill (ed.), *Leaves from the Notebooks of Lady Dorothy Nevill* (London: Macmillan, 1910), p. 127.
21   Elizabeth Ellen Buxton, *Family Sketchbook a Hundred Years Ago* (London: Geoffrey Bles, 1964), p. 39.
22   Valerie Belton, *The Norwich to Cromer Turnpike* (Norwich: V. Belton, 1998).
23   *Norfolk Chronicle*, 1862.
24   Buxton, p. 31.

2

The Maid of the Mill

In the intervening years between the coming of the railway to Cromer in 1877 and the arrival of Clement Scott in 1883, a number of public works had been added to the town. These included the opening of the waterworks, the building of the police station, the formation of the Fire Brigade and the building a new Wesleyan chapel. A New Cart Gangway to the beach was built and the old Lifeboat House pulled down. However, when Scott alighted at Cromer station, later known as Cromer High, he saw only open fields between the station and the centre of the town dominated by the church tower, the best part of a mile away. The town *was just a cluster of houses and cottages around the church, with scattered residences and farms.*[2]

The mediaeval town of Shipden, of which Cromer was a part, contained two churches. One was provided for the town proper, known as Shipden-Juxta-Mare. When this was in danger from being engulfed by the sea, Edward III granted permission for a new parish church to be built upon the site of an older church on higher ground in Shipden-Juxta-Felbrigg.[3] The height of the tower from ground level to parapet is 147 feet and from the ground to the top of the pinnacles, 160 feet, making it the tallest church tower in Norfolk. The question is often asked, why did such a small town boast such a magnificent church? Various answers have been suggested. One is that it was built over an extended period. Secondly, it is known from existing wills that it contained eight guilds or shrines. It is possible there were generous benefactors.

The town was clustered round the medieval church, bounded on the east by the Gangway and on the west by Garden Street. Immediately north of the church was Tucker Street on which was situated Tucker's Hotel. The High Street was a continuation of Tucker Street on the north west side of the church. Below the cliff stood the small jetty and

Louie Jermy stands facing her father, Alfred, the miller, who is leaning on the famous white gate. Sidestrand mill, symbol of Poppyland, dominates the scene.

promenade on which stood an extension to Tucker's Hotel and the Bath Hotel. The main road from Norwich swept down the hill into Cromer from the south, swung round past the church and left Cromer in a north-westerly direction, heading for Holt. There was some development south of this road and also along it to the west as it left Cromer. To the east of Cromer on the outskirts were several large houses at various times in the possession of Hoare, Buxton and Gurney families.

Among the landmark buildings still surviving that would have been seen in those days are Brunswick Terrace overlooking the gangway, the Hotel de Paris, The White Horse Inn in West Street, the Wellington Inn, Garden Street and the Albion Inn, Church Street. The main difference in Cromer between then and now, apart from the growth, is the fact that many old cottages and buildings in the town centre have been demolished to make room for road widening.

Scott described Cromer as he found it:

*In that red-roofed village, the centre of all that was fashionable and
select, there was not a bed to be had for love or money; all home
comforts, all conveniences were deliberately sacrificed for the sake of a
lodging amongst a little society that loved its band, its pier, its shingle
and its sea.*[4]

As Clement Scott noted the *fashionable and select* characteristics of
Cromer, it comes as no surprise that convention ruled polite behaviour:

*Custom had established a certain fashion in this pretty little watering-
place, and it was religiously obeyed; it was the rule to go on the sands
in the morning, to walk on one cliff a mile in the afternoon, to take a
mile in the opposite direction at sunset and to crowd upon the little pier
at night. But the limit was a mile either way. No one thought of going
beyond the lighthouse.*

Breaking with convention, Scott walked along the cliff top in the
direction of Overstrand. On reaching the lighthouse, he lay quietly on
the edge of the cliff among the ferns watching the children and adults
below him on the sand unselfconsciously engaged in playing tennis,
donkey rides and other holiday pursuits. Around him there was not
a soul in sight. It must be remembered this was before the golf course
was built and the countryside was more open than it is today with many
fewer trees. He was attracted by the silence:

*It is difficult to convey an idea of the silence of the fields through which
I passed, or the beauty of the prospect that surrounded me — a blue
sky without a cloud across it, a sea sparkling under a haze of heat; wild
flowers around me, poppies predominating everywhere*

He was drawn to the sight of the ruined Overstrand church tower
covered in ivy which he saw in the distance. As he neared Overstrand
a footpath led across the fields from the cliff top to the old Overstrand
Hall, and thence to the mediaeval ruined church. From there Scott could
either have walked down a footpath to Pauls Lane and up The Londs
or along the road from Cromer and thence into the village. He reached
the practically deserted village consisting of little more than thirty
scattered houses and found it deserted. The men were away fishing
and the women working in the fields. Scott realised there was no use
in looking for lodgings there and continued walking. It is impossible to

Louie Jermy poses by the porch of Mill House.

trace his exact steps today as part of the lane he travelled has succumbed to cliff erosion. Half a mile further on he turned a sharp left hand bend in the lane and came upon Sidestrand Mill House, which he described as *one of those farmhouses that is the exact reproduction of the style of cottage that all children are to draw when they commence their first lesson.* Scott was in fact looking at an attractive red brick building built onto the original cottage of knapped Norfolk flint. The old squints at the back bore record of smuggling days, but even the current miller at times flashed his red or green light according to circumstances.

As he stood leaning over a white gate surveying the scene, a girl appeared from the front door. Scott enquired of her, *could I be allowed lodging for a few days?* The time hallowed reply was, *indeed you could. Come in, sir.* She informed Clement Scott that her father was *the fortunate possessor of fast grey pony and basket chaise quite strong enough bring him over with his traps whenever he cared to order it.* That evening the miller conveyed Scott from *the monotonous existence of a seaside resort to the more simple pleasures of a sunny country life.* He records *we took a road that led through a wood, not quite deserted yet by the light, and passed one of the show cottages of the district, a gabled pleasaunce with a gothic porch, built in a hallowed clearance of some noble trees, sheltered by rhododendrons and azaleas and now showing an added charm owing to the lights in the latticed windows.*[5]

He arrived at the Mill House[6] that evening for a supper of eggs and bacon after this drive through the moonlit lanes. Louie placed Scott in the small bedroom above the front door, overlooking the central flower bed. He stayed in that room on every subsequent visit, and *would never*

The Mill House, 'the exact reproduction of the style of cottage that all children are set to draw when they commence their first lesson.' This postcard bears two Russian postmarks.

use any other, though it was a small room and more than half-filled by a half-tester.

The garden was noted for its beauty. A visitor arriving in mid-June left the following description:

> I have never been more enchanted; the roses are in full bloom, the scarlet and white shirley poppies, the cushion of poppies with their big heads are very gay. There is also red and white valerian, and purple Canterbury bells, Portuguese laurel with a creamy bloom. The roses and pinks are in full bloom — the windows you could hardly see for the rambler roses, pink and crimson. The lilies are almost ready to burst; the rooms are full of these lilies.

> In addition we have crimson foxgloves, fruit on the sycamores, and the honeysuckle on the wall. Apples are already large and the peaches on the wall against the wall as large as walnuts.

The lilac is out — the peonies are just over, as is also the yellow bloom of the burberry. The 'flags' or irises, which flank all the beds are just over. The syringa is about to bloom and the carnations are swelling. Sweet peas are in bud, and the creeping Jenny just finishing. The privet hedges are in full flower.[7]

The drawing room was on the left of the front door, where Scott did his writing.

A photograph of the drawing room as it was in those days suggests it must have been appalling in the excess of antimacassars, wax fruits under glass shades, countless portraits in home-made frames — scarcely room to stir without knocking some knick-knack off some impossible table. But, from all accounts, not a speck of dust anywhere; everything spotlessly clean and again one wonders how she did it![8]

The room on the right of the front door was the dining room with a long table in the centre capable of sitting twenty people.

Scott began his first full day at the Mill House with a bathe in the sea. He rejoiced in the remoteness and the solitude:

There is no bathing round the whole coast of England to be compared to the stretch of deserted virgin sand un-traversed by any human foot between the busy watering places of Cromer and Mundesley.

He relished the lack of constraints:

Three miles along the coast it would have been necessary to wait in turn for a bathing machine, to bribe the proprietor for preference, and to be strictly confined to the very proper regulations made at such places.

After breakfast the miller took Clement Scott to the upper storeys of Sidestrand mill which was a commanding landmark for miles around. It was sometimes known as the black mill as the exterior was tarred. The miller was Alfred Jermy who was born in Swanton Abbott.

He had a sensitive, questing face with a touch of breeding. He claimed a distant relationship with Isaac Jermy, Recorder of Norwich, who with his son was murdered in 1849 at Stanfield Hall by James Rush. He was a well known and well liked local figure and married four times.

In the days before mechanisation, a local windmill played a pivotal role in the life of the local community. For many years he worked the mill single-handed. He was every inch a true countryman. When Clara Watts

Dunton shook hands with him she commented *I felt the rough horny palm of this son of the soil between my fingers.*[9] Equally, he was intellectually curious.

The ten sided four-storey wooden mill was built over a brick base. Four double shuttered sails provided power for two sets of stones. The constant repairs were expensive, each wooden tooth in the big spur-wheel alone cost 3/6 to renew. It is recorded that *more than once with full power in the sails and all the machinery going, the sparks would fly and a bucket of water was needed to avert disaster.*[10]

In 1896 a severe storm wrecked two of the sails. The miller did not earn enough money and was too old to replace them. Five years later he lost the remaining two sails in a storm. Thereafter he merely bought and sold and stored his goods in the mill. Alfred Jermy retired from regular work nine years before his death. In old age *many hobbies and endless resources kept him happy, busy and contented,* even when walking became difficult. His garden was his chief concern. When walking became difficult he invented a tricycle for himself on which to ride about the garden. Alfred Jermy died on 29th October, 1913, aged 82

> ... *leaving his devoted daughter and companion, 'Louie of Poppyland', bravely facing the loss of material presence to find comfort in the spiritual one which is inseparable in her life. 'Aren't you lonely?' someone asks. 'Me lonely, with Daddy always here! never'. The bright face falls for a moment and the lips quiver slightly; but the cloud passes, and she brings out her books and newspaper cuttings and her treasured letters.*[11]

The mill fell with a mighty crash on 6th November, 1923, leaving a gap in the landscape never to be refilled.

From the top of the mill Clement Scott surveyed the scene. On one side were splendid views of a sparkling blue sea and on the other newly cut corn fields, looking golden in the summer sun. For the first time in many weeks the old mill was working as the new corn came pouring in. The miller initiated him into the art of making flour, bran and pollard. Clement Scott mused upon the ancient art of milling which had existed for hundreds of years and which was gradually dying out. The miller reminisced about the former days before mechanical binders broke the silence with the click, click of their revolving blades and when gleaning was still the custom. Industrious cottagers could glean enough corn for him to grind into flour that made a substantial reduction in their annual house hold expenses.

The girl who welcomed Scott as he leant over the white gate of the Mill House was Maria Louisa Jermy, invariably known as Louie. She was born in 1864, the second child

Miller Jermy on his home-made tricycle, circa 1910. , as featured in the Great Eastern Railway magazine.

of Alfred Jermy and his first wife, Cecilia, nee Colman, from Hunstall. There was an elder brother, William, born 1862.

Much of the information that has survived about her life is printed in a book entitled *The Maid of the Mill: Louie Jermy of Poppyland and Her Times, 1864 - 1936*. The book consists of reminiscences of Louie written by personages who knew her well. These were gathered together and published by Gwen Parry, who wrote the forewordrd. The print run was limited to a thousand copies. Today the book is scarce. Among the contributors were David Henry, Mrs. Clara Watts Dunton, (see Chapter 7), Dr. H.C. Dent, J. Jefferson Farjeon, Harry Farjeon, the leading lady Nellie Bonser, Mrs. E.E. Munnings, mother of Sir Alfred Munnings, and C.W. Barritt, J.P., C.C. These memoirs form a valuable source of information. However, memories are not wholly reliable and these must be treated circumspectly. There are a number of factual inaccuracies, not least in the first chapter entitled *The Birth of Poppyland and Louie Jermy as I knew her* by David Henry. He confuses Clement Scott's book *Blossom Land and Fallen Leaves* with *Poppy-Land*: Louie Jermy was the second child of Alfred Jermy, not the first: he is mistaken about the dates of the coming of the railway to Cromer and Clement Scott's death.

More reliable are the memories of Clara Watts Dunton. Mrs. Watts Dunton was the wife of Theodore Watts Dunton, who with the poet Algernon Swinburne were the first visitors to the Mill House after the publication of Scott's first article in the *Daily Telegraph* in 1883 (see Chapter 7). She had first met Watts Dunton as a sixteen year old school girl in 1892 when he was forty-nine and she was captivated by him. They were married in November, 1905, when he was 72 and she was 29.[12] Clara first met Louie Jermy in the summer of 1905 when she was staying in Cromer with her sister and family prior to her marriage in the November. She was joined by her future husband. One of their first expeditions was to Sidestrand where they had tea at the Mill House with Louie. From Clara's description of that first meeting we come as far as is possible today to catch a glimpse of the real Louie Jermy in her Poppyland days: her infectious enthusiasm; her warmth of heart; her solicitude for people; her sympathy and her boundless energy. *During the meal Louie hovered over us, attending to our wants, chatting merrily the while to Watts Dunton and casting towards us a look of benign interest.* On leaving, Louie presented Clara with a large bundle of flowers and Watts-Duncan with two little presents, one for Swinburne and one for himself. The latter turned out to be a small round wooden ointment box in which was placed a small doll dressed as a bride. On the box Louie had written, *Bachelor's Pill, One to be taken in a lifetime.* Clara was highly amused at Louie's sense of humour. She summed up Louie in the following words: *a woman of rare character was Louie Jermy, whose kindly spirit will long be remembered by all those with whom she was brought in contact.*

As the miller's daughter, Louie, like her father, was at the centre of the local community, where she more than ably fulfilled her responsibilities. Indeed, she became something of a legend. In the days when there was only one post, a letter could arrive between 10a.m. and 11a.m. announcing the imminent arrival of lodgers. Preparations had to be made quickly. Chickens had to be caught, killed and plucked, ready to be served up as a welcoming meal. Her blackberry puddings were famous. It has been recorded of her

> ... *as for the domestic side of life, there was nothing she could not do and do well. She baked and boiled, dug up potatoes from the garden, and often did her washing after her guests had gone to bed, and more than once she was surprised by the police, whose meeting place was at barn end, hanging out her washing at one o'clock in the morning.*

She was equally at home helping her father running the mill, as befitted a miller's daughter. If a storm was brewing she would race up the hill and unhook the sails if the wind was coming from a dangerous quarter.

> To talk about milling to Louie Jermy was a liberal education in itself. From the wheat chamber to the jumper, she would run through the whole gamut of stock, elam and gripe; clans, vanes and fliers; the torrent of words leaving he lips like the showers of sparks from 'the toes' when the machinery ran too fast.

Thus Louie Jermy, like her father, was a true child of the soil and intellectually curious.

> Louie Jermy was a link, not only between the past and present (in that mysteriously enthralling way appertaining to those who have had connection with the famous dead) but between the soil and the mind. There was in her the spirit of those whose work is the haul and the harvest, and of those who toil among words and images.[13]

These words were written by Harry Farjeon, who was a professor at the Royal Academy of Music. His brother, J. Jefferson Farjeon, wrote:

> Her literary phrases were a delight because they did not emanate from snobbery, but from sheer instinctive relish. She had the power to make you see what she described. She has made me see the dog Shuck performing his ghostly journey along the Overstrand road as I never visualised in the guide book. I have a vivid recollection of one evening when she described the smuggling days of her childhood. If I could convey in print the words as they came from her lips, accompanied by an eager intensity that wrenched you back through the years, I could make you shiver.[14]

The details of the movements of Louie Jermy are sketchy. Her mother, Cecilia, died before she was six. In 1871 Alfred married his second wife. She also bore him two children: a son in 1873 and a daughter in 1875.

> When the widower married again, and there was a little step-brother and sister in the home, the relations became strained; the high-spirited girl cut herself adrift for a while, and went to London, with two ladies of the theatrical profession, to one of whom she acted as dresser at Daly's Theatre. During this period Miss Charlotte Walters gave her lessons in elocution, and her lifelong interest in the theatre probably dates from then.[15]

However, Alfred Jermy's second wife died of consumption in 1875 and *Louie had come back to look after the children. That she went away again is certain, but exactly under what conditions is uncertain.*[16] This raises problems. The passing of the Elementary Education Act in 1870 set the framework for schooling of all children between the ages of 5 and 13 in England and Wales. Louie would have been thirteen in 1877, the year her step-mother died. Thus on this evidence Louie must have left home at a very early age.

David Henry, Mrs. Watts Dunton and Frederick Stibbons all state that at some time in her career Louie Jermy acted as housekeeper to Clement Scott. None of them, however, provide any dates or length of absence. Henry states that she left Scott to act as house-keeper to Sir Edward Burne-Jones, but Stibbons records she left Scott for the Pre-Raphaelite artist Henry Holiday. Stibbons is more likely to be correct, since for some time he spent many hours an evening with Louie taking notes of her memories. Moreover, when the old Sidestrand church on the cliff top was moved to a safer position inland, 1880–1, Sir Samuel Hoare employed Holiday to design the windows for the new building. It is known that Holiday stayed at the Mill House.

In 1880, Alfred Jermy had married a third time. *The new wife was a woman of more mature years, with a little money of her own; from all accounts somewhat prim and old-fashioned, and credited with having worn crinolines.* Alfred Jermy and his third wife together with all four children from the first two marriages were in residence at the Mill House when the 1881 census was taken. However, as Henry charmingly expressed it, *she was not long for this world.*

Spouse number four proved the least satisfactory of Alfred Jermy's four wives, and she eventually left the miller. Then Louie came home for good, and remained the prop and stay of the old Mill House to the end.

When the miller died in 1913, the tenancy of the Mill House and mill passed to Louie, but it was short lived. With the end of the First World War:

> ... *there swept that unfortunate aftermath of licence over the land that was the undoing of the old order. The 'bright young things' with their total disregard for proportion and good taste, made their influence painfully felt, and the character of Louie's guests changed.*

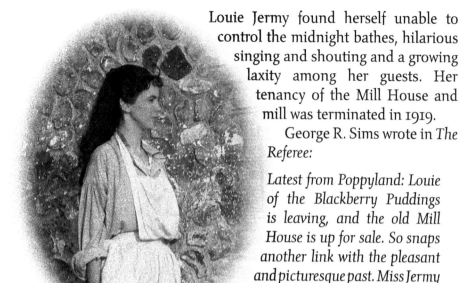

Louie Jermy found herself unable to control the midnight bathes, hilarious singing and shouting and a growing laxity among her guests. Her tenancy of the Mill House and mill was terminated in 1919.

George R. Sims wrote in *The Referee:*

Latest from Poppyland: Louie of the Blackberry Puddings is leaving, and the old Mill House is up for sale. So snaps another link with the pleasant and picturesque past. Miss Jermy should write her reminiscences. She has been the guardian home from home of famous men. I worked there with Wilson Barrett, with Henry Pettit and with Robert Reece. Alas, all three of my old friends are now at rest in the Garden of Sleep.

Phoebe Nicholls played the part of Louie in the BBC film 'Poppyland', first transmitted in 1985.

The sale of the contents of the house took place on 12th September. Lot 1 read *sundry brushes and dustpans.* The final Lot, 456, was *two hydrangeas in pots.* Louie withdrew many of the lots at the last moment and carried them upstairs. She must have felt that history, as well as her own life, were being uprooted. Mrs. E. E. Munnings, the wife of the miller at Mendham, Suffolk knew Louie. She wrote that on the day of the sale

I went to see her, nearly at the close, and found her in tears, sorting out the house-linen withdrawn, or bought in with a number of curios and some of her china.

I took her home with me to tea and later she went to her cottage in Tower Lane, which was filled with furniture![17]

Louie lived in this cottage in Tower Lane until the end of her life.

In 1923 she was visited by the leading lady, Nellie Bonser, whom she had first met in 1905. She left a description of her visit:

> Louie greeted me in Cromer, just the same sweet, contented soul as of old. I had my niece with me and we all went back to see her little cottage in old Tower Lane. What a change I noticed as we passed the old Mill House. One had to look beyond it to see it as it was in the old days. Inside Louie's cottage it was just like an 'Old Curiosity Shop'. She had everything around her — all her old memories. The little parlour was just a picture-gallery, photographs of celebrities of old days. We walked up to the 'Garden of Sleep', and how I missed the 'Old Tower!'

In1911 the sails of the mill had gone but it was still a place to be recorded in a photograph. In this instance it is the companion of the photographer, Nellie, in the picture.

In the evening Louie came for a short way back with us and for the first time I saw tears in her eyes, but the last goodbye wave had a happy smile to accompany it.[18]

In December 1925, the cottages in Tower Lane were struck by lightning. Louie lost most of her collection of newspaper articles she had carefully preserved. She lived on contently with her memories, hoping to meet her step-brother who had long lived in California.

Today she is just remembered by very few, in old age pushing a dilapidated pram round the village selling vegetables and sifting for cinders from the village rubbish tip for her fire. The excitement of her brother's homecoming caused her to have a stroke which proved fatal. She died in 1934 and was carried to her grave in Sidestrand churchyard by four Overstrand fishermen.

Clement Scott's visit to the Mill House in August 1883, was the first of many. He referred to himself as *one of the warmest admirers of Cromer,* adding, *I cannot believe that this corner of England, which to me of all corners of the earth smiles most, will ever be spoiled, disfigured or vulgarised.* To fully understand the reasons for Scott's attraction and devotion to *this corner of England*, it is necessary to do so against the background of his career and first marriage, to be considered in the following chapters.

1   Alfred Collison Savin, *Cromer in the County of Norfolk: a modern history* (Holt: Rounce & Wortley, 1937).
2   Martin Warren, *Around Cromer* (Stroud: Alan Sutton, 1995), p. 9.
3   Savin, p. 4.
4   Clement Scott, *Poppy-land,* 4th ed. (Norwich: Jarrold, 1895), p. 6.
5   North Repps Cottage.
6   By 1886 the Mill House had come to be called Poppyland Cottage (Ordnance Survey 6-inch map).
7   Gwen Parry, *Leaves from an Overstrand Scrapbook* in Cromer Museum, CRMMU 1981.52.1.
8   Gwen M. Parry, *The Maid of the Mill: Louie Jermy of Poppy-land and her Times, 1864–1934* (Westminster: Gwen M. Parry, 1936), p. 12.
9   Clara Watts-Dunton, *The Home Life of Swinburne* (London: A.M. Philpot, 1922), pp. 185–6.
10 'The Old Miller of Sidestrand and Poppyland', *Great Eastern Railway Magazine,* 1919, pp. 14–16.
11 'The Old Miller', p. 14.
12 Watts-Dunton, p. 15.
13 Parry, *Maid of the Mill,* p. 42.
14 Parry, *Maid of the Mill,* p. 39.
15 Parry, *Maid of the Mill,* p. 3.
16 Parry, *Maid of the Mill,* p. 11.
17 Parry, *Maid of the Mill,* p. 44.
18 Parry, *Maid of the Mill,* pp. 45–46.

3

Clement Scott's Career

Clement Scott was a man of his age, whose character was forged by Victorian values. He experienced a typical middle upper-class upbringing, with a powerful and successful father, a loving mother, a much loved nanny, unhappy early schooling, followed by a public school education. His father was the Reverend William Scott, Perpetual Curate of Christ Church, Hoxton, 1839–1860. He was born at the Parsonage, New North Road, Hoxton, into a family of several brothers and sisters on 6th October, 1841. Clement Scott called himself *a strange, rather silent, introspective and thoughtful boy*. He recorded that *in the very two places where character is said to be formed — home and school — I was least understood.*[1] His father, as well as being a parish priest, was a brilliant journalist with a marvellously accurate mind, a power of close argument and of marshalling facts, and a storehouse of learning. He wrote for the *Saturday Review* and social leaders for the *Morning Chronicle*. Had any of his sons shown the least ambition to follow in his footsteps, he would soon have been put in his place. Scott had to conceal his journalist ambitions from the whole family, apart from his *dear mother,* who was sworn to secrecy. Thus from an early age he was inhibited from expressing his innermost feelings.

Three events in his childhood played their part in influencing him to become a dramatic critic. Very early in life he was sent to a day school in Islington whose Head Master was the celebrated school teacher George Darnell, 1798-1857. Clement Scott recalls: *I hated life at this terrible Islington school. The head master frightened me to death, and I regarded him, rightly or wrongly, as some awful ogre.* On the way to school Scott had to walk past 'Dodd's Dust Heap' which he found a *paralysing horror* as an army of hideous women dressed in hats and coats like men sifted rags and bones. As the young Scott walked along Eagle Wharf Road, over

Britannia Bridge and across Shepherdess Fields, he records between *the moment I closed the door behind my home in the New North Road, to the instant I put my hand on the latch of that beastly school door,* he turned his attention to gaily coloured theatrical posters covering the walls and tried to imagine what the plays could be about. *This was my self-invented game of imagination to change the blackness, the dullness and the despair of my miserable life.*

In 1849, at the age of eight, Clement Scott was taken to see his first play. Previously he had been taken to the pantomime in company with others, but on this occasion he was taken by two members of his father's parish as a special treat. It made a profound impression on him. The memory remained for over fifty years. He later wrote, *it sealed my fate.*

A journalist needs descriptive powers and a retentive memory. An example of Scott's descriptive powers and memory may be seen in his account of this visit to the theatre written many years later. It began with a visit to Dolly's Chop Shop situated in a court just of fNewgate Street. Scott recalled:

> ... *a glass cupboard stocked with the most presentable raw chops and steaks that eye ever rested on, all neatly trimmed, pared, and ready for cooking. The customer or guest arriving at Dolly's was greeted by a cook in a snow-white cap and apron, holding a fork, with which the visitor promptly speared the chop or steak that took his fancy, and then and there he transferred his prize to another cook stationed at the 'grid', who, according to instruction, grilled the delicate morsels under your nose.*

> *The repast was enjoyed in cosy boxes, with oyster sauce of the very best; and the good brown stout or London porter in polished pewters were draughts to be remembered.*

He recalled the interior of the Theatre Royal:

> *Very little luxury; no lounging stalls; the pit right up to the orchestra; the faithful pitties sitting on hard benches, and constantly disturbed between the acts by women with huge and clumsy baskets filled with apples, oranges, nuts, ginger beer, bottled stout and bills of the play, which they offered to the public in shrill discordant voices - the very descendants of Nell Gwynne herself.*

Scott continued his education at Marlborough College. In the holidays, on the pretext of wishing to become a diligent student of Shakespeare, he was allowed to make frequent visits in both summer and winter holidays to the *Princess's Theatre*, Oxford Street. He was encouraged by his father who presented his son with a copy of Shakespeare bound in Russian leather, which he kept all his life. These visits to the theatre proved useful when he returned to Marlborough after the holidays. At the Shakespeare readings after chapel, Clement Scott was usually presented with the best parts as he had

> ... *seen them acted, heard the intonations of the voices of the great actors, and noted their style. From that moment, Scott records, the dream of my life was not to become an actor; no! such an idea never entered my head for an instant, but I did earnestly desire to qualify myself for the post of dramatic reviewer of players and plays.*

Having passed the competitive Civil Service examination, Scott began work as a clerk in the War Office on 23rd May, 1860 when he was eighteen years old. He was appointed to the post by his father's old friend the Right Hon. Sidney Herbert, later Lord Herbert of Lea. It was Derby Day. Scott described the scene as he walked down Regent Street:

> ... *the horns were blowing, and the coaches and carriages, with postilions in white beaver hats and blue jackets, were dashing past me. The girls were all smiling; the hampers with goodies and champagne packed up behind, were swinging behind the rumble. If ever I experienced the joy of living , I did so on that glad May Day.*[2]

Scott had intimated to his father that he might go down to the Derby. His father strongly advised him not to do so:

> ... *take my advice and don't go down to the Derby. The Chief Clerk at the War Office has written to ask you to report yourself in Pall Mall on the 23rd. If he had meant the 24th he would have said so.*

Scott was glad he followed this advice. By preferring the War Office to the Derby he was placed over the heads of six brother competitors who preferred Epsom Downs to Pall Mall. In later life that seniority of a few hours *meant promotion, in advance of six good men quite as good, and perhaps better,* than himself, wrote Scott. On his arrival at the War Office, Scott

... was escorted down stairs to a room facing the pavement in Pall Mall with a large plate-glass window. I was planted down to a desk and set to work at once copying draft letters, indexing pay-lists, and registering dead soldiers' effects.

His salary was £150 per annum, paid quarterly. Scott remained at that job until he retired with a pension in 1879.

At the start of his War Office career Scott had two pieces of 'good luck', as he called them. The first was to find himself sitting opposite Tom Hood, who was the son of the celebrated poet Thomas Hood. They soon formed a strong friendship. Tom Hood, who had to work hard for a living, gave Scott much encouragement. He corrected Scott's early attempt at poetry and encouraged him by printing his contributions for publications called *Fun* and *Saturday Night*, of which he was editor. W.S. Gilbert was another contributor.

His second piece of 'good luck' was to be elected a member of the Arundel Club at an early age. In 1861 the Club had moved from its old home in Arundel Street, Strand, to 12, Salisbury Street, Strand, overlooking the River Thames. Here Scott met

... the flower of Bohemia Land in those days, Bohemian actors, Bohemian authors, Bohemian barristers, artists, men of science and solicitors — all the very pick of the basket.

Even at his early age, Scott was friendly with many of them. He appreciated this varied company. He saw it as a *universal provider of all good things — knowledge.* There, Scott wrote, he *spent some of the happiest days — and I fear nights also — of my life. I have never mixed in any society where conversation was so general or so good. It was an education in itself.* The Chandos Club was celebrated for its large upstairs rooms in which, *perhaps, more thoroughly jovial suppers were eaten than in any other club in London.*

Early in his career at the War Office Clement Scott had acquired the nickname 'Kitten' on account of his playful and spitfire temperament. On one never-to-be-forgotten day, Tom Hood looked across the desk, with his gold eyeglass in his eye, and said: *have you heard, Kitten, that Foard is going to resign the Sunday Times. There will be a vacancy, you know, for a dramatic critic.* Scott recorded: *my brain seemed to reel.*

At that time the *Sunday Times* and the *Era*, apart from the 'dailies', were the plums of the profession. Through his friendship with the owner and editor, Frederick Ledger, Scott was already contributing small reviews to the *Era*. Ledger is reputed to have said of Scott: *I have discovered, I think, a very promising recruit. He is ambitious, industrious, a tiger for work, but, dear me, he requires a deal of editing.* This experience with the *Era* increased Scott's confidence.

Scott was so desperate to become dramatic critic of the *Sunday Times* that he took the step, unheard of in those days, of obtaining testimonials from the influential friends of his father. He received letters from the Duke of Newcastle, Lord Herbert of Lea and Lord Robert Cecil, later Lord Salisbury, and Alexander James Beresford Hope. But Scott had also applied for a testimonial from a friend who was a Freemason. He handed Scott the important document which was adorned with signs and symbols he did not understand. Scott handed it to the editor of the *Sunday Times* who was also a Freemason. Scott never discovered which of the two sets of testimonials was the more influential, but at the age of twenty-one he was appointed dramatic critic to one of the most influential theatrical and trade papers in London, at the princely salary of £2 a week.

In his life-long connection with the theatre, Clement Scott strove for two reforms: *Free Trade in Drama; Independence of Journalism* and other criticism. However, when he was appointed dramatic critic of the *Sunday Times*, a protectionist policy was in force. The proprietor took the view that to mention a French or foreign play in any shape or form was to insult our own actors and *take the bread out of their mouths*. The memory of one of the most serious riots in the history of the British stage was still very fresh. This took place on 12th June, 1848, at the Drury Lane Theatre, which dared to put on the French play, *Beau Geste*. Rabid protectionists screamed, *take it away, kill it, bury it, crucify it*. Italian effeminacy and French immorality were accused of crushing Shakespeare. The complaint was that the most sacred domain of the British actor and author had been invaded. As dramatic critic of the *Sunday Times* Scott was expected to follow an editorial policy with which he was strongly at odds. However, he would not yield to protectionist coercion. In 1865 he was told his services were no longer required. By 1868 he was tired of being freelance and picking up commissions as they occurred His ambition was to be appointed dramatic critic of the *Weekly Dispatch*.

Once again Scott recalled that luck aided him in his ambitious enterprise. A very old and dear friend told him that a share in the *Weekly Dispatch* had been bought by a solicitor in the City with whom he was closely connected and that he would effect an introduction, if Scott wished. Within a short while Scott had been confirmed in the appointment he so coveted. When Scott joined the *Weekly Dispatch*, it earned him many enemies as he was considered an interloper for daring to combine journalism with his daily work at the War Office. However, he was at last free to seek to implement his second ambition for the theatre, independent criticism.

At the time of being appointed dramatic critic of the *Weekly Dispatch*, Scott described the conflict facing an independent critic, which haunted him all his life:

> *The tone of independent criticism, which the public desires, and the theatrical manager as well as the artist hates; the criticism that the reader of the newspaper, who has seen the play, considers absolutely fair; but that the person criticised very often, and perhaps naturally so, considers unfair and unjust; is the kind of criticism that brings the grey hairs of the critic in sorrow to the grave.*

Years later, Scott returned to this theme when he was dramatic critic of the *Daily Telegraph*. On Sundays afternoons the proprietor, J.M. Levy, frequently sent for Scott to read the notices before they were 'set up' and talk things over with him. Scott recorded:

> *At any extra stinging passage he would wince as if the pain had been inflicted on him personally, and then, with one of his delightful chuckles, teeming with humour, would say: 'It's God's truth, Clement, — it's God's truth — but it will hurt the poor thing so — can't you — can't you tone it down a bit?*

Scott wrote of those days that no amount of work frightened him. In addition to his daily work at the War Office he was at the theatre every time a new play was produced, he was contributing several columns a week for the *Weekly Dispatch*, he was sub-editing and writing for the unsuccessful *Morning Summary*, as well other smaller commitments. It comes as something of a surprise that in 1868 Scott married his first wife (see Chapter 4). By this point of his career Scott was gaining a reputation.

Within three years of his marriage he won three new appointments. In June 1870 he was given absolute control of the dramatic department by the proprietor of a new daily newspaper, the *London Figaro*. He wrote under the *nom-de-plume* 'Almaviva'.

Scott's next major appointment was, in his words, *another lucky turn in fortune's wheel*. Late one Saturday evening he was enjoying supper at the Chandos Club having completed a review of the first night of an important new play. Across the smoke filled room he saw the editor of the *Observer* making his way towards him. It transpired his dramatic critic had nothing to say about the play. He asked Scott to write a small piece. It was now nearly 2 a.m. The deadline was 3.30 a.m. Scott set to work once he reached the

Clement Scott, aged 26, two years before his marriage to Isabel du Maurier

Observer's office. Long before the paper went to press Scott had written a complete criticism about a column and a half in length. Next morning the editor sent for him and offered the post of dramatic critic on the *Observer* — one of the plums of the profession.

In 1871 Scott was sent for by J.M. Levy to visit him at his office in Peterborough Court, Fleet Street. Levy was the principal proprietor of the *Daily Telegraph* with sole control over the musical and dramatic departments. Levy asked Scott if he would like to join the staff of the *Telegraph* as an assistant to the critic who had served the paper with distinction for many years. He was assured he could continue writing for the *Observer*. Scott continued to do so until he retired from the *Observer* in 1873. He continued working for the *Telegraph* until 1898.

In 1892 Clement Scott embarked on a world tour during the course of which he married an American journalist, Constance Margaret Brandon, in San Francisco following the death of his first wife in 1890.

In December 1897 Scott contributed an article for an obscure Evangelical periodical entitled *Great Thoughts* on the topic of the propriety of women taking a career on the stage. He made it clear he was *referring to that which goes on behind the scenes*, suggesting it was really *impossible for a woman to remain pure who adopts the stage as a profession*. There was much more in similar vein. Scott had no idea his views would be made public. When they appeared in the daily press they caused a national outburst and brought Scott considerable unpopularity.

The *Daily Mail*, the *Daily Telegraph's* rival, dredged up Scott's past indiscretions. This is relevant in so far as it affected his first marriage and thus the history of Poppyland. On April 7th, 1898, the *Daily Telegraph* published an apology from Clement Scott:

> *Referring to the interview with me, and published in* Great Thoughts, *in the December of last year, I desire to express my regret to the ladies of the theatrical profession, and to the theatrical profession at large, for having given utterance to words which I now realise must have inflicted pain upon many good women, whom I not only respect, but whose claims to the good opinion of all I freely and frankly avow.*

But by then the damage had been done. Scott resigned from the *Daily Telegraph* in December, 1898.

Clement Scott died impoverished at his home in Woburn Square in 1904 after a long illness. A group of the acting profession, including Sir Henry Irving and Herbert Beerbohm Tree, staged a benefit for him at His Majesty's Theatre on 23rd June, 1904. The *Tatler* commented:

> *It is tragic to reflect that the quick brain and the good heart may never again be used in the service of the art which he loved so long and so deeply. The stage owes an immeasurable debt of gratitude to Clement Scott and that the players are not ungrateful is proved by the splendid programme, headed by Sir Henry Irving, which has been organised by way of appreciation of a critic of sterling worth and a man whose worst fault was impulsiveness.*

Scott died two days later and is buried at the convent of the Sisters of Nazareth at Southend-on-Sea for whom he undertook much charity work. His appeals for Christmas hampers for cripples were legendary.

This brief outline of Scott's career as a dramatic critic cannot begin to convey the pressure, opposition and emotional strain under which Scott was working for most of his life, nor his vast output. He covered in his own words:

> ... at full length every important pageant, royal marriage, royal funeral, reception, cricket match, race meetings at Epsom, Ascot, Goodwood, Doncaster and Newmarket; Oxford and Cambridge boat race, Henley Regatta, and innumerable exciting events of daily London life; descriptive holiday articles by land and lake and 'poppy land' and sea.

In addition, he published several volumes of poetry.

When he was appointed dramatic critic of the *Weekly Dispatch* in 1868, he recalled it led *to the earliest of the stormy days* of his career, in which there were many lawsuits. When writing for the *London Figaro* Scott recalled *I was putting my head into a 'hornet' nest, but I did not flinch, though the pain I suffered from time to time was indescribable.*

His trenchantly expressed views inevitably made him many enemies. His second wife wrote that his *enemies were countless, but with his back well against the wall, he launched out right and left. There wasn't one critic with him in the struggle.*[3] Publications were threatened with the loss of advertisements if they persisted in printing support for a free trade and freedom of expression for critics. However, Scott was strongly supported by the editors of the *Weekly Dispatch*, the *London Figaro*, the *Observer* and not least by J.M. Levy, proprietor of the *Daily Telegraph*. Scott had the highest regard for Levy and looked upon him as his best friend.

At the height of his career, Clement Scott was regarded as the foremost critic of his day.

> The eternal cry of the heart could be heard in every notice Clement Scott ever wrote of the theatre. His love and passionate worship for the stage was indeed so powerful that he compelled attention whenever he wrote about it, and created an enthusiasm which became not only contagious, but infectious — and his following grew, and grew and grew, until he absolutely voiced public opinion as regards things theatrical.[4]

His incisive reviews brought the art to new heights. He was the first critic to review opening nights, much to the chagrin of some producers.

> His notices of new productions were so definite, so convincing, so boldly

stated, so fearless and incisive, so analytical and accurately estimated, that they read as if he had put himself in the position of plaintiff, counsel for the defence and judge , too. He weighed this side and the other, he gave his reasons why, and why not, and after thoroughly probing into the minutest detail pronounced sentence accordingly, and nine hundred and ninety times out of a thousand his followers declared his judgement to be theirs.

In his lifetime, Scott changed the public perception of the acting profession.

I don't suppose anyone except 'the man in the know' can possibly realize with what desperateness and earnestness Clement Scott fought single-handed to attain the present — and I hope lasting — popularity and importance of the theatre and theatrical profession. He raised a once despised trade into a fine art, and placed it on a singularly high platform.

This came at some physical and emotional cost to Clement Scott.

When plays finished occasionally at eleven-thirty, or eleven forty-five, or even later, as the case might be, it required pulse, and life, and energy, to sit down and pour out a boiling column — perhaps more — on to sheet after sheet of blank paper, to hear the compositors' boys, as I have heard them, pounding down the corridor to fetch the 'copy' as soon as it was written- and until it appeared in the paper later in the morning. He never arrived back before 2 a.m.[5]

These reviews were eagerly read by producers, actors and actresses and play-goers alike later that morning. Some actors waited up all night for the paper to be delivered. There is a story about one actress calling at his chambers in Lincoln's Inn Fields and saying, 'Mr. Clement Scott, my carer will be made or ruined tonight; do tell me if your criticism is likely to be favourable.' In reply he handed her a penny saying, 'Dear lady, buy a copy of the *Daily Telegraph* tomorrow morning and you will have my answer'.

1   Clement Scott, *The Drama of Yesterday & Today* (London: Macmillan, 1899), 2 vols.
2   Scott, *Drama*, vol. 1, p. 355.
3   Margaret Scott (Mrs. Clement Scott), *Old Days in Bohemian London: recollections of Clement Scott* (New York: Frederick A. Stokes Company, 1919), p. 8.
4   Scott, *Old Days*, p. 7.
5   Scott, *Old Days*, p. 9.

4

Clement Scott's Marriage to Isabel du Maurier

Clement Scott loved women:

> If it be a gift to think of lovely girls and women whom we have worshipped in early life, only in their first youth, only in the pure charm of their earliest influence, only when they were 'queen roses of the rosebuds, gardens of girls' — then this happily is a gift that I for one possess, and which I seriously endeavour to cultivate.[1]

Before reaching the age of twenty-one, Scott had converted to Roman Catholicism. On 30th April, 1868, he married Isabel Louise Busson du Maurier at the Brompton Oratory. Isabel was the grand-daughter of the most notorious courtesan of her time, Mary Anne Clarke. Mary Anne was the mistress of Frederick, Duke of York, brother of King George III and Commander-in-Chief of the British Army. He set her up in Gloucester Place in 1803. Mary Anne wisely kept the Duke's letters to her. When amid much scandal the relationship inevitably broke down she sold the letters back to the Duke for a lump sum of ten thousand pounds, and an annuity of four hundred pounds for herself, and two hundred pounds each for her two daughters, Louise and Ellen. She left England to live on the continent, when Ellen was nine.[2]

In 1831 Ellen, at the age of thirty-one, was swept off her feet by the charm of Louis-Mathurin du Maurier. Louis-Mathurin was a man of many talents and a scientist but one whose inventions inevitably came to nothing. Like his father, he was irresponsible with money, speculating with what money that did come his way. During the twenty-five years of marriage he and Ellen were never far from poverty. Ellen's annuity was invaluable throughout her life.

Louis-Mathurin and Ellen had three children: George, born 1831, Eugene 1835 and Isabel Louise, 1839, who married Clement Scott. When his father died in 1856, George abandoned his unhappy career as a scientist. He borrowed £10 from his mother and fulfilled a long-time ambition when he went to Paris to train as an artist. From there he moved to Brussels.

In the summer of 1858 he suddenly lost the sight in his left eye and was fearful of losing the sight in the other. Isabel's best friend, Emma Wightwick, whom George du Maurier later married, told the family of a celebrated oculist near Düsseldorf, where there was also a school of painting. Thence he and his mother and Isabel moved in the spring of 1859.

In 1860 George du Maurier was visited in Düsseldorf by his old friend the budding artist Tom Armstrong. Part of the reason for the visit seems to have been Tom's attraction to Isabel, which attraction, however, was not reciprocated. Armstrong suggested that he and George should travel to London where he, Tom, would give George some useful introductions. They set out together, leaving Ellen and Isabel to trudge home in the rain to their lodgings.

After an early struggle, George du Maurier found success. Following the death of the celebrated *Punch* cartoonist John Leech on 30th October, 1864, at a meeting held at the Bedford Hotel, Russell Square, on 1st November, George du Maurier was appointed to the staff of *Punch* magazine. As long as his other eye held out, his future was assured. He was the friend of many well-known writers and artists. His marriage to Emma Wightwick was happy and fulfilling. He became a well-known novelist, the author of *Trilby* and other novels. A grandson was the model for J.M. Barrie's *Peter Pan*. He was the grandfather of the novelist Daphne du Maurier. He died a wealthy and respected man.

While George was working hard to establish himself in London, Ellen and Isabel were living in straightened circumstances in Düsseldorf. Isabel was happy in Düsseldorf: *no place could suit me more,*[3] she wrote to her future sister-in-law. Her brother wrote to his mother: *Düsseldorf must be very agreeable to Isabel as she is made so much of there.*[4] He wrote to Isabel: *you are surrounded by very nice people of which you are the particular pet.* Isabel was flattered by a German prince. She made friends among the English community and German princelings while she looked for a husband. Unfortunately, neither they, nor her family, had any money. Isabel had a long-standing affair with a young man called Samuel Perrot, which became a family joke. It would appear that Samuel was too diffident or too fond of his *unconscionable Mamma* to propose marriage. George du Maurier wrote from England to his mother in Germany:

> *Isabel's love affairs seem to run smooth enough; I send you a little sketch which I flatter myself is very good, shewing[sic] Isabel and Samuel 20- years hence, waiting to be married till he has provided for his sister's grandchildren.*

Isabel du Maurier, Scott's first wife, in a rare depiction. She is playing the piano, with George du Maurier shown amongst his artistic friends prior to his wedding to Emma Wightwick, seated centre. George is reading, facing her. James Whistler sits on the floor to the right.

Isabel du Maurier comes down through history as a person of some character. She is recorded as scolding the servants when aged six. She was a fine pianist, but did not always keep up with her practice. An extract from a letter she wrote to Emma Wightwick on Emma's engagement to her brother George provides an insight into the playful aspect of her nature:

> Pray give me an account of yourselves, how many a times a week you tiff and make it up. Whenever I want to get anything out of Kicky I see I must ask his verlobte,[5] and from the state of his heart, I should say he would do it par express, whatever the request. So to begin with, dear Emma, do lecture your brautigam[6] about not writing often enough to his unfortunate and forgotten sister. I expect a very long letter from you, by return of post in the form of 'Consequences' — Who the gentleman was? Who the lady was? Where did they see each other? What he said to her? What she said to him? What the consequence was? and what the world said?[7]

In 1851, Isabel, then aged twelve, had attended the wedding in Boulogne of her uncle, George Clark, to a young wife, Georgiana. On this occasion she also met her grandmother, Mary Anne Clarke. Neither Mary Anne nor Georgiana were a good influence on the young Isabel. In April, 1861, George Clarke died. The young widow was left with a small son. They came to stay in Düsseldorf for a year with Ellen and Isabel, who *enjoyed her position as a belle of Düsseldorf society.* In Bonn Georgiana was extravagant and enjoyed flirting with German officers, to the neglect of her son. Isabel and Georgiana became inseparable. *Isabel was only happy when she was surrounded with people. She could not bear being by herself, and found pleasure only in talking and living in a crowd.*[8]

Ellen and Isabel finally moved to London in 1865. Isabel's romance with Sam Perrot appeared to be over and she probably agreed to accompany her mother who wanted to live near George. It is known that Clement Scott contributed poetry to *Punch* magazine. It seems likely that Clement Scott and Isabel met through her brother's connection with the magazine.

Scott was a typical Victorian man with behind him the stability of a male dominated Victorian society, as shown above. Many of his happiest days were spent in the Chandos Club in male company. His mother, to whom he was devoted, was the archetypical Victorian wife. Her place was in the home supporting her busy and successful husband, supervising the running of the household and rearing her children with the help of a nanny. It is difficult not to conceive that Scott envisaged a similar wife. Scott has left to posterity a list of the qualities he admired and looked for in women: *love, loyalty, homage, or respect.*[9] He wanted a wife who would adulate him and place him at the centre of her life. As he grew to know the du Maurier family, Scott might have hoped that his marriage would share some the qualities as that of his brother-in-law, George du Maurier and his wife, Emma, who was

> ... *an unfailing companion, always at hand and with no interests outside her home life. Placid in temperament, nothing seemed to move her strongly or excite her. She literally waited on her 'Kiki'[George] hand and foot, each and every day, and lived only for him and his children.*[10]

While holding down a full time job at the War Office, Scott was totally dedicated to the theatre for which, he said *he never lost his first love,* since attending his first play. In 1868, the year of his marriage to Isabel, Scott wrote,

> *I was struggling for the stripes of a non-commissioned officer having risen from the ranks. I was tired of being a free lance, weary of 'develling' for my friends.*

He continued:

> *No amount of work frightened me in those days. I was at my desk at the War Office all day; I was sub-editing and writing for the Morning Summary; I was at the theatre whenever there was a new play, and I was contributing my several columns to the Weekly Dispatch. I cannot tell you how many failures in the way of newspapers I helped to start.*[11]

In his words at this time, *I was a glutton for work.* It was always likely he would place work before the demands of his marriage. It is a wonder he found any time for Isabel.

Edward Seago once commented on a painting that if the figures were put in

> ... *merely to add interest to the picture, they will probably fail to take their rightful place. Those who labour on the land, are not like actors who make an 'appearance' on the stage.*[12]

In writing of the farm labourers in Norfolk Scott showed little understanding or sympathy for the poverty in which they lived. They were merely adjuncts in his descriptive picture. It must be open to question how far he understood or sympathised with Isabel and her needs. It may well be asked, would she take her *rightful place* in the marriage? It is unlikely he would be able to provide the company and companionship she needed.

Isabel, on the other hand, would never be able to be the kind of

wife which Clement Scott craved. It was outside her experience. Isabel was no Emma Wightwick. Isabel had always lived an insecure and uncertain life, often on the verge of poverty. On one occasion Ellen complained Isabel was so weak from bad nourishment she could not study the piano properly. On another occasion while living in Düsseldorf she could not attend a party through lack of a tarlatan. She was pretty and vivacious and used to the attention and flattery she had experienced at Düsseldorf. George wrote in May, 1861, that *Isabel would die of ennui* in village

Scott at 50, from a feature article in the Strand *magazine*

life. In the same letter he wrote, *Isabel would be an immense pet with my fellows — she has the gift of pleasing to a great extent, and uses it.* Isabel needed attention, amusement and a social life. When Shirley Brooks, the future editor of *Punch*, heard of the engagement, he wrote in his diary on 14th August, 1867, *I hope it is a hopeful match, it can't be more.* He recognised the incompatibility between their respective backgrounds and their differing expectations of the marriage.

The fear that Shirley Brooks expressed in his diary was only too prescient. Any hopes that *Isabel would provide warm and adoring female companionship were rudely shattered.*[13]

> *Their union was not a very happy or smooth one, and little frowns of worry appeared on her face when her children were quite young. Like all Victorian women, she hid her sorrows with a brave face.*[14]

This implies that Isabel made an effort and to some extent accepted her position within the marriage. This is what was expected of Victorian wives at this time. *It was correct to be blind and dumb, and to see or speak was an offence against the laws that governed the behaviour of her class.*[15] However, towards the end of her life Isabel eventually left Scott and his succession of mistresses and returned more and more to Düsseldorf, the only place she had really been happy. George du Maurier's son-in-law wrote that Isabel was

> … *an extremely witty woman with a rather sharp tongue, whereas her husband was of a very sentimental nature, on account of which he was subjected by her to a great amount of chaff. This difference led to their estrangement, so a friendly separation was arranged, she keeping charge of the four children, two boys and two girls.*[16]

To sum up: at the time of their marriage Scott was 27 years old and Isabel 29. Each had a well formed character forged both by their respective backgrounds and their vivid experiences of life. These, no doubt, reinforced their preconceived ideas of what they were hoping for from the marriage. Neither had the experience to give to the other what they were looking for. We can only guess or speculate the reasons why Isabel *chaffed* her husband. Whether it was his philandering, or shortage of money, or the fact that Scot may have placed his work before Isabel, the cause of the breakdown would seem to be that neither was able to fulfil the expectations the other brought to the marriage.

In 1882 Clement Scott published a book of poems, *Lays of a Londoner*. It concludes with a poem entitled *To Isabel*:

> *For years, twice seven, we've boldly struggled through*
> *The thorny thicket of a tangled life;*
> *When all grew dark, hope came at last from you,*
> *Most placid woman and most perfect wife!*
> *Aw'd by its lovely majesty I've seen*

God's star of beauty in your eyes.
What sweeter than yours has ever been!
What grander gift — a love that never dies.

Trembling I ask how dared I pluck the flow'r,
Your lily-life of modesty supreme,
To water it with tears and sorrow's show'r,
To give love's passion, and to take love's dream?
What have I ever asked you never gave?
When smiled you not at life, though overcast?
Your love is one forgiveness — spare me! save
The real present from the pictured past!

The evidence is circumstantial, but bearing in mind the date of Clement and Isabel's marriage was 1868, *twice seven* years previously, it is difficult not to conclude that this poem refers to their marriage. If that assumption is accepted, it confirms the conclusions reached above: the marriage was a struggle; Isabel tried to fulfil the role of a Victorian wife, for which she was ill suited; Clement Scott was asking forgiveness for his unfaithfulness.

It is likely the separation occurred about this time. The following year Scott came to Cromer and Poppyland came into being. Dr. Dent recorded that Louie Jermy told him Scott spent New Year's Eve for fifteen consecutive years in the Garden of Sleep, the old Sidestrand churchyard. Whatever the truth of this, he could hardly have done so if living with a wife.

A letter written to her sister-in-law, Emma du Maurier, by Isabel is dated *Sept. 23.* Presumably it was in 1890 as she was seriously ill. This letter is important in the context of Isabel's life for two reasons: it shows her bravery in the face of adversity and her willingness to make the best of difficult situations; it shows, too, that Clement Scott was still concerned about her:

Dear Emma,

I have been too bad to write to anyone and am not any better - as I daily get weaker and my sight is failing me — To-morrow another doctor, or rather physician, is coming in from Plymouth, as my doctor

here wishes it and Clement too — I have neuralgia pains all over me —
it is like rheumatic fever without the _fever_ — consequently I have been
much injected with morphia, hence my bad sight, coupled with extreme
weakness — Whatever I look at is blurred and doubled and it makes me
swear inwardly but copiously.

Well, I suppose I shall get better in time — Torquay for a fortnight
would pick me up, as it is all sunshine and bath chairs, but at present I
cannot move — however, enough of me and my ailments.

Directly after Christmas I must try and let the house and get away for
Jan. Feb. and March, if possible — However sufficient unto the day,
and by that time I may be strong and hearty or under the sod.

Isabel Scott died on 26th November, 1890 at St. Barnabas Cottage
Hospital, Saltash, Cornwall. Her death certificate recorded death due to
Meningitis and Exhaustion. Her death was recorded without feeling in
the _Cornishman_ on 4th December:

SCOTT — No. 26 Tamar Bank at Saltash, Isabel (nee Busson du
Maurier), wife of Clement Scott of 52 Lincolns-inn-fields, London.

The marriage of Clement Scott and Isabel du Maurier is of interest
in this context in only so far as it affects the history of Poppyland. It
is clear that by the time Scott visited Cromer in 1883, just seven years
before Isabel's death, the marriage was to all intents and purposes over.
If the marriage had not failed, history might have taken a very different
course. Indeed, the term Poppyland might never have been invented.

It is against his background of a life spent in feverish energy, late nights,
controversy and fighting causes, together with his aggressive nature,
coupled with a broken marriage this and the previous chapter have
portrayed, that the intensity of Clement Scott's love for the remote peace
and beauty of this stretch of the north Norfolk coast can be understood.
The absence of the Overstrand fishermen at sea and their wives working
in the fields in harmony with nature as he walked through the village on
his initial visit, was in stark contrast to the bustling scenes of a London
street. The controlling influence in the lives of these rural workers was
nature's timetable of tides and seasons. The fishermen were bound by
the weather and the natural daily ebb and flow of the tide, while Scott's

Mill House from the rise on which the mill stood.

life was governed by the daily flow of commuters streaming in and out of London. The lives of the agricultural workers were governed by the four seasons. In Norfolk he saw all around him unspoilt nature; in London he daily encountered urbanisation. The controlling influence in Scott's life as theatre critic was to meet an artificial deadline in a newspaper office, the lives of these rural workers were governed by nature's rhythm.

Clement Scott's love for Cromer and Poppyland stands apart from all his other writing.

It was his intensity of feeling for the peace and beauty of Poppyland that is so evident in Scott's articles: *the country around is in full glory of summer loveliness;* and *seldom has the late autumn shone upon English rustic life with more beauty than on the year that is now passing away.* Light figures prominently in his descriptions: *the lover of all that is picturesque in nature can revel in the tricks of colour and light.* He refers to the sunlight *on sea and cliff;* to light *dancing down the deserted lanes,* and light *travelling fast over fern-covered hills.* He extols the *golden light* as the sun goes down on the harvest field.

He compared living in the country to living in a cramped city. In the latter, the country is imported into the city by teams of wagons of market gardeners, by caged larks singing by back doors, by flowers in Covent Garden market and by grass visible through palings of closed London squares. In the country all these are to be found unfettered in their natural surroundings.

Scott's articles in the *Daily Telegraph* were subsequently collected and published in book form. The late Fred Stibbons recounted how it came to be written:

> The story of how the Poppyland Papers came to be written I had from Louie's own lips. She was a great reader of newspapers and she had cut out each article by Scott as it appeared, tying them together with a pink ribbon.

> On one of Clement Scott's weekend visits he asked for a loan of the cuttings. He promised her great care would be taken of them and that she would have them back. She knew no more until the book appeared that made her and the old red [sic] mill famous all over the world.[17]

The book was published with the permission of the editor of the *Daily Telegraph*, J.M. Levy. Louie possessed a first edition of Clement Scott's *Poppy-Land Papers* inscribed:

> To Louie Jermy, without whose kindness, affection and sympathy, Poppy land, its peace and pleasures, would have been an unknown region, and no paradise to Clement Scott, 16th November 1885.

This inscription illustrates the depth of gratitude that Clement Scott recognised towards Louie Jermy for revealing to him the *paradise* he christened Poppyland. It is arguable that her character held as much hold over him as did the peace and beauty of Poppyland itself. It is impossible not to notice the contrast between the domesticity and the infectious simplicity of Louie Jermy in her desire to please, and the *chaffing* of Scott's wife, which is said to be the cause of the breakdown of the marriage. Louie gave Scott the *loyalty, homage, respect,* he craved. Arguably Louie Jermy was no less influential in making Poppyland world famous than was the writing of Scott himself.

Poppy-Land Papers proved to be an immense success. On 5th September, 1890, the *Morning Post* reported:

> Mr. Clement Scott is to be congratulated upon the success of his 'Poppy-Land'. It is only three weeks since Messrs Carson and Comerford, the publishers, issued a second edition. This is already exhausted, and a

third edition of 5,000 copies is in the press for issue next week.

This would seem to suggest the fame of Poppyland had become well established by 1890. The fourth edition is dated 1894. There were at least twelve editions.

However, the most intense expression of Clement's Scott love for Poppyland in his writing is to be found in his poem *The Garden of Sleep* to be considered in the next chapter.

1   Clement Scott, *Ellen Terry: an appreciation* (New York: Frederick A. Stokes Company, 1900), p. 1.
2   Leonée Ormond, *George du Maurier* (London: Routledge & Kegan Paul, 1969), p. 6.
3   George du Maurier, *The Young George du Maurier: letters, 1860—67* ed. Daphne du Maurier (London: Peter Davies), p. 48.
4   Ormond, p. 162.
5   German for engaged girl.
6   German for bridegroom.
7   George du Maurier, p. 48.
8   Daphne du Maurier, *The du Mauriers* (Harmondsworth: Penguin, 1949), p. 299.
9   Scott, *Ellen Terry*, p. 2.
10   C.C. Hoyer Millar, *George du Maurier and Others* (London: Cassell, 1937), p. 33.
11   Clement Scott, *The Drama of Yesterday & Today* (London: Macmillan, 1899), vol. 1, p. 535.
12   Edward Seago, *A Canvas to Cover* (London: Collins, 1947), p. 23.
13   Ormond, p. 200.
14   Daphne du Maurier, p. 311.
15   E.F. Benson, *As We Were* (London: Hogarth Press, 1985), p. 86.
16   Millar, p. 82.
17   Parry, *Leaves.*

5

The *Garden of Sleep* and the Aesthetic Movement

A short distance beyond the Mill House in Sidestrand was Tower Lane, which led towards the cliff top. At the far end of Tower Lane stood the deserted church tower of the former Sidestrand church. The cliffs on this part of the north Norfolk coast are liable to erosion. Such had been the scale in the nineteenth century that in 1881 it was considered expedient to pull down the existing Sidestrand church and rebuild it further inland adjacent to Sidestrand Hall. At the behest of Trinity House, the old tower was left standing as a navigational aid to vessels.

When Scott first visited the site, the graveyard was tumbling over the edge of the cliff and the area was covered in bright red poppies swaying in the breeze. The location and the circumstances greatly appealed to his romantic imagination which led to his celebrated poem *The Garden of Sleep*. The date is unknown, but a date of 1885 has been suggested. The poem was first published in the *Theatre*, of which Clement Scott was the editor. It quickly reached the attention of actors and actresses and other members of the theatrical profession. It greatly helped to spread the knowledge and fame of Poppyland.

When set to music by Isidore de Lara, it reached a far wider audience. For this reason it might be easy to dismiss *The Garden of Sleep* as nothing more than a passing popular song. However, when it is considered within the context of Scott's life and the cultural life of the era in which it was written, it will be seen there were a number of external influences at work in its creation.

In 1890, Clement Scott described his reason for writing *The Garden of Sleep*.

The Garden of Sleep, Sidestrand. 'On the grass of the cliff, at the edge of the steep, God planted a garden, a garden of sleep.'

The spot is so eminently picturesque — a deserted churchyard among the cornfields, a garden of sleep among the poppies; it is so impressive on the brightest day in summer, so still on the calmest moonlight night, that on one occasion I conceived a song suggested by the situation and its surroundings. I pictured a solitary man standing in a churchyard, surrounded by sea, cliff and villages and poppies, waiting for and lamenting the loss of the woman he loved.[1]

He makes it clear that *a garden of sleep may mean a churchyard and that a poppy has been called a symbol of death*. The poem reads:

THE GARDEN OF SLEEP: A SUMMER SONG

On the grass of the cliff, at the edge of the steep,
God planted a garden — a garden of sleep!
'Neath the blue of the sky, in the green of the corn,
It is there that the regal red poppies are born!
Brief days of desire, and long dreams of delight,

They are mine when my Poppy-Land cometh in sight.
In music of distance, with eyes that are wet,
It is there I remember, and there I forget!
O! heart of my heart! where the poppies are born,
I am waiting for thee, in the hush of the corn.
Sleep! Sleep
From the cliff to the Deep!
Sleep, my Poppy-Land,
Sleep!

In my garden of sleep, where red poppies are spread,
I wait for the living, alone with the dead!
For a tower in ruins stands guard o'er the deep
At whose feet are green graves of women asleep!
Did they love, as I love, when they lived by the sea?
Did they wait as I wait, for the days that may be?
Was it hope or fulfilling that entered each breast,
Ere death gave release, and the poppies gave rest?
O! life of my life! on the cliffs of the sea,
By the graves in the grass, I am waiting for thee!
Sleep! Sleep!
In the Dews of the Deep!
Sleep! my Poppy-Land,
Sleep!

Whenever this poem is read today, on the internet or in a written publication, it is done in the above version. Crucially, Scott's own introduction is frequently omitted:

Wherever men are noble, they love bright colour: and wherever they can live healthily, bright colour is given them in sky, sea, flowers, and living creatures.

Ruskin, 'On Poppies.' [Proserpina]

These few words change the whole tenor of the poem from what became a popular song into verses of deeper thought and significance. The words are a quotation from John Ruskin's highly subjective treatise

One of many pictures of the tower in Sidestrand Garden of Sleep. The particular interest in this image is that it shows the rebuilt Sidestrand church in the background.

on flowers which he called *Proserpina*. In classical mythology Proserpina was the daughter of the Roman goddess Ceres, goddess of agriculture, grain crops and fertility.[2] While gathering flowers, she was abducted into the underworld by Pluto where she was held captive. She was allowed to return to her mother in the spring, but had to return to the underworld in the autumn. In spring, when Ceres receives her daughter back, the crops blossom. In autumn when Proserpina returns to the underworld Ceres changes the leaves to shades of brown and orange, which are the favourite colours of Proserpina, as a parting present. At one time red poppies grew abundantly in cornfields and for that reason since time immemorial the poppy has been considered Proserpina's flower. Proserpina's association with flowers was inseparable from her rule over the spirits of the dead.[3]

The poppy was the first flower Ruskin described in his *Proserpina*, and with good reason.

> The book is in part a tribute to James Ruskin [Ruskin's father] and a lament for the lost security of family life. But the myth of Proserpina had acquired a meaning still closer to Ruskin's emotions. He saw Proserpina as an image of Rose de la Touche. The course of his hapless love for the Irish girl has a pervasive effect on his botanical studies.[4]

For John Ruskin, there was therefore an element of autobiography in his *Proserpina*. It has already been noted that Clement Scott prefaced his *Garden of Sleep* with a quotation from *Proserpina*. This inevitably raises the questions about Clement Scott: was there also an element of autobiographical truth in the *Garden of Sleep?* At the time Scott wrote the poem his marriage was breaking up. In all probability he was no longer living with Isabel. Even though he might not recognise the fact, is it possible Scott himself was sub-consciously *waiting for and lamenting the loss of the woman he loved?* When he wrote in the second verse the line *Did they love, as I loved, when they lived by the sea,* does it refer sub-consciously to his love for Isabel? Indeed, is it possible Scott could have written this poem, divorcing himself completely from his life? Perhaps these are questions that can never be answered, but in so far as *The Garden of Sleep* spread the fame of Poppyland, they are not irrelevant.

Algernon Swinburne said the title Scott gave to the area of *Poppyland* was *highly aesthetic.*

It can be plausibly argued that *The Garden of Sleep* shows strong aesthetic influences. Intellectual or artistic movements do not spring out of nothing. There are usually antecedent influences. *John Keats was a major influence on the English aesthetic movement*[5]. He wrote of the opiate effect of poppies, inducing drowsiness and sleep:

Or on a half reap'd furrow sound asleep
Drowsed with the fume of poppies, while thy hook
Spares the next swath and all its twined flowers.[6]

This is a theme running through the aesthetic oeuvre. Thus the poppy came to be seen as a symbol of the aesthetes, with the lily and the sunflower. In the comic opera *Patience*, which seeks to ridicule the excesses of the aesthetic movement, the poppy is singled out for mention, together with the lily:

Though the Philistines may jostle, you will rank as an Apostle in the high Aesthetic band,
If you walk down Piccadilly with a poppy or a lily in your mediaeval hand.

References to the *aesthetic movement* are commonplace, but there was no unified or organised movement as such. The later aesthetes may be thought of not as a *coherent group but as a* mood, *affecting large numbers of people.*[7] To the best of the author's knowledge it has never been suggested Clement Scott was considered by contemporary society to be among the aesthetes, but on his own admission he was *mad about blue china*[8] *and* he associated with known *aesthetes* or admired their work, including Algernon Swinburne, the poet of aestheticism. Scott referred to Swinburne's *Midsummer Holiday*

in the following words: *But why say much more of a place that has been immortalised by such a coiner of sweet words and such a singer of the sea as Algernon Swinburne?* Oscar Wilde, the arch-apostle of aestheticism, greatly admired Clement Scott:

In the days when Wilde spent most of the year at Oxford as an 'undergrad', he used frequently to write to Clement Scott in the most modest terms of humble adulation.
He had almost a reverence for the art of acting even then, and several of his college essays on plays and players were printed in the Theatre magazine.[9]

Algernon Swinburne, sufficiently intrigued to explore Poppyland for himself.

Among the well known actresses who were considered to be *aesthetes* were Ellen Terry and Lillie Langtry, both known to Scott. Scott wrote a little known appreciation of Terry. There are two positive references to Scott in Langtry's autobiography, *The Days I Knew.* She secured a part in the play *Peril* by Scott. Strangely, there are no references to Lillie in Scott's semi-autobiography. Lillie Langtry was also a friend of Oscar Wilde. She devoted several pages to him in her autobiography. Lillie Langtry claims that the well-known line from the opera *Patience*, quoted above, *If you walk down Piccadilly with a poppy or a lily in your mediaeval hand*, refers to their friendship:

Before Oscar had achieved celebrity, and was unconsciously on the verge of it, he always made a point of bringing me flowers, but he was not in circumstances to afford great posies, so, in coming to call, he would drop into Covent Garden flower market, buy me a single gorgeous amaryllis (all his slender purse would allow), and stroll down Piccadilly carefully carrying the solitary flower. The scribblers construed this act of homage as a pose, and thus I innocently conferred on him the title 'Apostle of the Lily'.[10]

Ellen Terry, herself a visitor to Poppyland, in the role of Guinevere in 'King Arthur'.

Another characteristic of the aesthetes was intensity of feeling. In 1879 *Punch* published a George du Maurier cartoon of a young woman with a typical pre-Raphaelite face gazing up earnestly at a man with a supercilious expression on his face, to whom she has just been introduced. The caption reads: *ARE YOU INTENSE?* Intenseness of feeling was part of the creed of the aesthetical movement: *the strict Aesthete admires only what in his language is known as intense.*[11] The language of Scott's The Garden of Sleep is at times deeply intense, as exemplified in such expressions as *brief days of desire* and *long dreams of delight*. These are also expressions of deeply felt escapism, which itself is a theme of the aesthetes.

The aesthetes came to express their feelings and intensity in exaggerated mannerisms and pretentiousness. This did not pass unnoticed. Gilbert and Sullivan's opera *Patience* is a parody on the aesthetes. D'Oyly Carte wrote of the aesthetes in 1881:

The 'movement' in the direction of a more artistic feeling, which had its commencement sometime since in the works of Mr Ruskin and his supporters, doubtless did much to render our everyday existence more pleasant and beautiful. Latterly, however, their pure healthy teaching has given place to the outpourings of a clique of professors of ultra refinement, who preach the gospel of morbid languor and sickly sensuousness — tending to an unhealthy admiration for exhaustion.[12]

On 16th August, 1887, the *Norwich Argus* published a long article headed *MR. G.R. SIMS IN 'POPPYLAND'*. George R. Sims was a well known journalist and play-wright and one of the earliest visitors to the Mill House. Much space is devoted in this article to describing how the whole atmosphere of Poppyland is conducive to sleep and exhaustion.

You can drop off to sleep in Poppyland, I assure you. Poppyland is called not only because of the red flowers that grow so luxuriantly around, but because the air is an opiate that sends everybody off to sleep, man woman and child. If there were enough inhabitants in the district to make a chorus, the chorus they would sing would be, 'We're all nodding.' The animals get drowsy here as soon as they are born. The inhabitants are never really wide awake, and efforts made by visitors to keep their eyes open are ludicrous in the extreme. The strong air affects all who come within its influence. Nature is perpetually waving a chloroformed handkerchief in the faces of the Poppylanders, and there are few who can fight off the drowsiness which steals over them

Towards the end of his article, Sims says he is in the same room and sitting at the same table on which Swinburne wrote *A Midsummer Holiday* and Clement Scott wrote *Poppyland Papers* in the Mill House. He, too, is writing a poem called *The Garden of Sleep*, as a lampoon upon Clement Scott's poem of the same title. The article by Sims is the final proof linking *The Garden of Sleep*, and hence Poppyland, to the aesthetic movement.

In the garden of sleep, on the crown of a cliff,
Where the breezes blow in with an opiate whiff,
I lazily lay on my side in the sun
From the dawn of the day till the daylight is done.

A somnolent silence my soul stealeth o'er
As the wanton waves whispering woo the shy shore,

And the slumber of sleep of the stillness is borne,
Where the pretty pink poppies camp out on the corn.

The buzz of the bee as he hums in the bush,
The glow of the gold and the purple and plush,
The rose in its riot of rapturous rest
All sang me to sleep as a babe at the breast.

Then wafted and winged on the
  ambient air,
Through the ivory gate float the
  phantasies fair,
The dreams of delight of the
  drowsiness born
Where the pod of the poppy is
  crushed in the corn.

From the dawn of the day till the
  dusk and the dark
To the hoot of owl from the lay of
  the lark,
I have slumbered and slept on
  this Lethe-laved land
Where the succulent seaweed
  sings songs to the land

And now, as the midnight moans
  out on the mere,
It seems in my dreams that a
  murmur I hear;
'Tis a bibulous boatman, who
  says with a sniff,
'O crime and O crikey, a corpse on the cliff'.

A very formal image of lampooner, playwright and journalist Geeorge Sims from the book 'Good Old Gaiety' by John Hollingshead.

He labours to lift me — a stagger, a screech!
And two bodies lie battered and bruised on the beach;
The rude rocks re-echo the thunderous thud,
And the boulders and billows are blotted with blood.

I chide not the churl lying flaccid and flat,
But I dreamingly, dazily say. 'Who was that?'

Then I pule , in a pang of papaverous pain
'You have waked me too soon. I must slumber again.

The references to both Scott and Swinburne in these lines are evident. Swinburne was *the great aesthetic poet.* The use of the word *opiate* in the second line *and the pod of* the *poppy crushed in the corn* may possibly refer to drug taking. As the Aesthetes were playfully debunked in a series of cartoons in *Punch* by George du Maurier, and pilloried in both F. C. Burnand's play *The Colonel* and in Gilbert and Sullivan's opera *Patience* so too, in his article and poem Sims is somewhat playfully debunking aestheticism and the Garden of Sleep.

1   Clement Scott, *Blossom Land and Fallen Leaves* (London: Hutchinson, 1890), p. 213.
2   The probable origin of her name is the Latin proserpere 'to emerge', referring to the growing of grain.
3   *New Approaches to Ruskin: thirteen essays* ed. Robert Hewison (London: Routledge & Kegan Paul, 1981), p. 145.
4   *New Approaches*, p. 145.
5   Leonée Ormond, *George du Maurier* (London: Routledge & Kegan Paul, 1969), p. 245.
6   John Keats, 'Ode to Autumn'.
7   Ormond, p. 247.
8   Clement Scott, *Ellen Terry: an appreciation* (New York: Frederick A. Stokes Company, 1900), p. 101.
9   Margaret Scott (Mrs. Clement Scott), *Old Days in Bohemian London: recollections of Clement Scott* (New York: Frederick A. Stokes Company, 1919), p. 238.
10   Lillie Langtry, *The Days I Knew* (London: Hutchinson, 1925), p. 89.
11   Walter Hamilton, *The Aesthetic Movement in England* (London: Reeves & Turner, 1882; 3rd ed. reprinted by Pumpernickel Press, 2011), p. 50.
12   Diane Canwell and Jonathan Sutherland, *Pocket Guide to Gilbert and Sullivan* (Barnsley: Remember When, 2011), pp. 62–63.

6

The Influence of Lord Suffield of Gunton Hall

Situated in park land six miles south of Cromer, in the parish of Gunton, is a large estate once belonging to the Harbord family. The size of the estate varied over time between 17,000 and 12,000 acres, part of which included what later became known as Poppyland. In 1742 on inheriting Gunton Hall from his maternal uncle, Harbord Harbord, William Morden, who was born at Thorpe Hall, changed his name by Act of Parliament to William Harbord. He shortly set about enlarging the old hall under the direction of the architect Matthew Brettingham into a fine Palladian stately home. In 1746 he was created a baronet. His son, Harbord Morden Harbord, was created the first Baron Suffield in 1786. The Barons Suffield exercised considerable influence over the development of the general area, and later of Poppyland, until the commencement of the first world war.

Through marriage the family inherited the large manor of Gimingham-Lancaster. The second Baron acquired the manor of Cromer Gunners in 1815. In 1820 Lord Suffield built a Marine Villa on the cliff top at Cromer overlooking the existing jetty. In 1830 this property and two other pieces of land were put up for auction, but failed to find a buyer. The cliff top residence was then rented to Pierre le Francois[1] who opened a boarding house which he called the Hotel de Paris. Pierre rented it until his death in 1841. His widow, Mary, continued to run it until her death in 1845. The Estate finally sold in the 1860s. The small villa was extended westwards and another hotel next to it was incorporated into it. The Hotel de Paris, with its dominant position in the town centre overlooking the pier, and still in existence today, played an important role in the history of Cromer and Poppyland. It housed many famous guests. Edward Harbord, 3rd

Baron Suffield, 1781 — 1835, was a radical British politician who took a leading role, among others, in the successful campaign to abolish slavery in the British Empire and was also a prison reformer.

Of particular importance was the network of friendships built up by the fifth Baron, Charles Harbord, which helped to create social stability in the area. Close to Gunton is the substantial estate of Felbrigg. This was inherited by Vice Admiral William Lukin in 1824 (see Chapter 1). Vice Admiral's Lukin's daughter, Cecilia, married Henry Baring as his second wife in 1824. Cecilia rented Cromer Hall from her sister, Maria Augusta, who had inherited it from her deceased first husband, George Wyndham of Cromer Hall. Henry and Cecilia's only daughter, also Cecilia, married Charles, 5th Lord Suffield, in 1854. Cecilia's brother, Edward (Ned) became the first Lord Revelstoke and head of Barings Bank. A further son, Evelyn, 1841-1919, became the first Earl of Cromer. He spent the much of his childhood at Cromer Hall until 1852 when the Countess sold the hall to Benjamin Bond Cabbell.

The second of Lord Suffield's influential friendships was that with Edward, Prince of Wales, later King Edward VII. As a boy, Charles Harbord went for a walk in Hyde Park with his brother-in-law, George Anson, C.B., who was a member of the royal household. There they encountered, probably by design, the young prince, a little younger than Charles, and his tutor. This was the beginning of a life-long friendship during which they were often at each other's side. Charles became a Lord-in-Waiting to Queen Victoria. When the Prince had finished his education he was placed in the army and Charles was invited to become his chaperone. It is said, apocryphally, that at the end of the audience the Queen said to Charles Harbord, *my son shall have everything he wants.* Charles took this instruction rather too seriously. As a young officer he accompanied Edward to the fateful summer camp at the Curragh in August, 1861.

When he was approaching his twenty-first birthday Prince Albert and Queen Victoria decided the Prince of Wales needed a country house of his own *and one situated far enough away from London to keep their erring son on the straight and narrow.* Lord Palmerston suggested an 8,000 acre shooting estate in Norfolk belonging to his son-in-law, known as Sandringham. Although the asking price was high, this suggestion was accepted. Prince Albert died before the negotiations began, but the

Queen was anxious to see her late husband's wishes fulfilled and the deal was completed. There are suggestions that Lord Suffield had often extolled the beauties of Norfolk to his friend, the Prince of Wales, who was anxious to buy Gunton Hall. Although at this time neighbouring Blickling Hall was Harbord property, it was entailed away from the family and thus Gunton was not for sale.

In 1861 Edward, Prince of Wales, became engaged to Alexandra Marie Charlotte Louise Julia, daughter of Prince Christian of Schleswig-Holstein-Sonderburg-Glucksburg. The royal couple needed a home. The marriage took place in 1863, which was also the year Alexandra's father became King of Denmark.

Lord Suffield wrote:

After he [the Prince of Wales] came to Sandringham I saw a great deal of his Royal Highness. He frequently came over to Gunton for the shooting, and I met him, too, at other houses where we were guests together. In one way or another I saw the Prince and Princess constantly, and the friendship that had begun in his earliest childhood, and which continued until his death, grew very close and strong during those days in Norfolk.[2]

When Sandringham House became too small for the growing family of the Prince and Princess of Wales, it was decided to replace the mansion at Sandringham with something more suitable to the needs of the Prince and Princess. Prior to completion in 1870, the Prince and Princess leased Gunton from Lord Suffield to be closer to Sandringham. Gunton became the centre of much social activity and *rowdy shooting parties. In one period of just four days, 3,207 head of game were shot.* A photograph survives showing the Princess of Wales practising archery with Lord Suffield with a cricket match in progress .

In 1868 Lord Suffield was appointed Lord-in-Waiting to the Prince of Wales. He retained this post until 1872, when he was appointed Lord of the Bedchamber to the Prince, a post he held until 1901. He was sworn of the Privy Council in 1886. He was Chief of Staff to the Prince of Wales during his visit to India, 1875–76. On the accession to the throne of the Prince of Wales's in 1901, Lord Suffield became Lord-in-Waiting-in-Ordinary to the king. He retained this post until the King's death in 1911.

A third friendship of Lord Suffield's which had a considerable bearing

At Gunton Hall, circa 1870. It is suggested that Lord Suffield is instructing the Princess of Wales in archery, whilst the Prince looks on.

upon the future of Poppyland was that with Cyril and Constance Flower, later Lord and Lady Battersea. In 1877 Constance Flower, as she was then, paid a visit to Gunton Hall. She recalled:

Lord Suffield always faultlessly attired, a courtier, the bienvenu of Sandringham and Marlborough House, an adept at sport of all kinds, remained unfortunately for his own dignity and happiness of others, too young in tastes and proclivities for his years.[3]

Significantly, Lady Battersea added: *some members of that family I look upon as my personal friends.* Lord Suffield himself recognised the importance of these personal relationships.

It is always gay and cheerful, though the kind of excursionist that patronises Blackpool and Margate, fortunately for Cromer does not appreciate our little town, and the big houses in the neighbourhood contribute largely to the society and general cheeriness of the place.

This friendship resulted in Lord Suffield offering Cyril Flower the option to purchase two adjoining villas in the village of Overstrand.

Lady Battersea recorded:

> On one never forgotten day Lord Suffield suggested to Cyril that he should consider the purchase of two villas adjoining one another and belonging to him. They were standing on about three acres of ground in the small seaside village of Overstrand, which then numbered about thirty houses, and within two miles of Cromer. I had no idea then that I was looking at my future home. But having decidedly refused to become the owner of Desdemona's Palace in Venice, and after having heard, much to my relief, that Sheringham was out of the question, I felt that Cyril, in all fairness, ought to have a free hand in the choice of his future domicile.

These properties were later enlarged into the Pleasaunce which played a crucial role in the history of Poppyland (see chapter 8).

It is difficult for us today to understand the magnetism that royalty once exercised upon the upper classes and aristocracy. The memoirs of a Gentleman-Usher at court of St. James illustrate this:

> Only those who have had to control crowds can understand that occult impulse which turns civilized people into a herd in the presence of royalty.[4]

Entertaining royalty and keeping up with the Marlborough Set was expensive. In 1865 the Prince of Wales paid a five day visit to Gunton Hall from Monday to Saturday, during the course of which 524 bottles of wine were consumed, including whisky 10, gin 10, rum 6, cherry brandy 5, Madeira 12, Chablis 6; Curacao 2; Monsey, pale and brown 28, various sherry 197; best port wine 36; various Champagne 117; various red wine 89.[5] Lord Suffield is recorded as saying:

> I do not think I was even personally extravagant and certainly I never gambled in any shape or form but somehow our expenses generally exceeded our income.[6]

It has been written from the mid-1870s, England's landed gentry suffered a debilitating sequence of events which amounted to a severe agricultural depression. Their incomes were diminished; the inherited privileges of the aristocracy were being eroded by a new burgeoning middle and upper class. Lord Suffield was not immune from the effects of these changes.

In the early 1880s he leased Gunton Hall to Mr. E.M. Mundy of Shipley Hall, Derbyshire. Mundy paid a *big sum* for the lease. In addition he gave the game to Lord Suffield to cover the cost of rearing it. In 1882, while Mundy was there with a large house party, the hall was badly damaged by fire. One day in December the library chimney caught fire. The fire was extinguished, but very early the next morning smoke was seen issuing from a corner of the house. The beams running through the chimney had smouldered and started a fire. The flames destroyed one wing with the largest bedrooms and reception rooms below. Many valuables were saved, but the library containing many old books and family papers lost together with pictures, costly pieces of furniture and other items that could never be replaced. When Lord Suffield reached the scene from London in the afternoon he saw *a hideous, gaping, blackened ruin.* He recorded in is memories:

> *Billy Keppel, who was one of Mundy's guests, had had a narrow escape. He was sleeping in the burning wing, and when he awakened he made for the door, but the fire had already gained such a hold that he was driven back by the smoke. Happily, his apartment had a second entrance, and he came out by that, but just as he left the room the floor fell in.*

At some time in 1870s Lord Suffield had built a dower house on the edge of Overstrand on the Overstrand Road, which he named Carrington Villas. It was later re-named Harbord House. The dates are uncertain, but it was possibly as a result of the difficulties large landowners were facing, or the fire at Gunton, that Lord Suffield recalled in his memoires, *I have not been to Gunton for many years now.* Referring to Cromer, he wrote, *we lived a good many years in the house I built there.*

It was at this time that Lord Suffield needed to exploit his land in Cromer and Overstrand. For this he needed good rail communications. He was well acquainted with the benefits a rail connection could bring. He was present at the opening of the first railway to be built in Norfolk in 1844. This was the Yarmouth and Norwich Railway. He recorded:

> *I distinctly recollect the excitement over the first train that left Thorpe Station for Yarmouth in 1844, when I was fourteen. A brass band occupied the carriage next to the engine, and the rest of the train was filled with guests invited by the directors.*

The through railway line from London to Norwich via Ipswich opened in 1849. However, this did little to ease the difficulty of travelling to Cromer by rail as it still entailed riding on a coach between Norwich and Cromer.

Progress in building a railway towards the coast north of Norwich was slow, due to a number of reasons. The sparse population did not offer the promise of large profits. There was competition and rivalry between the North of Norfolk Railway and the East Norfolk Railway. Bankruptcy and death also played a part in the delays. In 1867 Lady Suffield cut the first sod of a projected line from Whitlingham Junction to North Walsham. Little work had been completed when the contractor died, and work on the line halted. With the cessation of work, there was a cessation in buying shares of the company. It was as a result of this that Lord Suffield and the Directors of the Great Eastern Railway met at London in 1869 to try and resolve the problem. New contractors were appointed and more money raised. The eventual opening of the East Norfolk Railway's line to North Walsham took place in October, 1874. An extension to Cromer had to be postponed owing to lack of capital.

Concerted efforts were made to raise more capital. The local interest was almost entirely from large landowners who stood to benefit most. Lord Suffield, Benjamin Bond Cabbell of Cromer and Upcher of Sheringham all subscribed. Messrs Gurney & co. took £5,000 of shares. Local landowners between North Walsham and Cromer sold their land cheaply. They co-operated in other ways by permitting of removal of ballast from their land and the setting up of on-site brick works when brick earth was discovered at North Walsham, Antingham and North Repps. The line to Gunton was eventually opened on 29th July, 1876. The line to Cromer opened a year later.

Much of the land east of Cromer belonged to the manor of Gimingham Lancaster which Lord Suffield owned. By 1877 it had good rail communications which were improved ten years later with the opening of Cromer Beach station (see Chapter 7). In 1887, Lord Suffield saw a chance for development:

Then I turned my attention to Cromer and Overstrand, where there was, as yet, nothing to attract visitors. Anyone going to Cromer now, after being away for thirty-five years, would scarcely recognise the place. It was then simply a village, with a few houses on the hill belonging to the county people, who only used them in the summer, and Overstrand was merely a hamlet.[7]

Lord Suffield was responsible for the first substantial new building in Overstrand since the arrival of Clement Scott. This consisted on a row of terraced houses today known as 12-18 Harbord Road. It is unclear whether these were built following Lord Suffield's need for money following the fire at Suffield or the beginning in the rise of the popularity of Poppyland, or a combination of both.

On 13th Monday, June, 1887, under the heading *AUCTION SALES TO-DAY*, the *Morning Post* carried the following advertisement: *BAKER*

and SoNs,[sic] at Cromer - One hundred Plots of Freehold BUILDING LAND, at 1.30 for 2.30. Purchase money could be paid in *easy instalments* and free conveyance was offered. This advertisement in a national newspaper is an eloquent testimony to the extent to which Cromer had become well known. This development became the modern Suffield Park estate.

In 1888 Lord Suffield auctioned of 88 plots of land, including provision for recreation and lawn tennis, at Overstrand. Had the plans for this fully materialised, Overstrand would have been a very different village. The fact

Charles Harbord, 5th Lord Suffield, photographed by local and London photographer Olive Edis.

they did not do so is largely due to the fact that Lord Battersea purchased much of the land that would have been affected. The map accompanying this proposal shows that Lord Suffield had already built a row of villas in Pauls Lane and Harbord Road.[8]

A further sale of land took place in Overstrand in June 1897 when 89 plots of freehold building land were offered for sale in the parishes of

Overstrand and Sidestrand. The auctioneer pointed out that

> ... the sale of the estate offered a unique opportunity to those who are
> desirous of erecting residences here, since nearly the entire village of
> Overstrand, with the exception of the land now offered, is in the hands
> of the landowner.

He continued by saying that

> ... he had never had an opportunity of putting up an estate which
> offered greater signs of increased value than the estate they were now
> disposing of. At Cromer people had bought land for £60, and had sold
> the same plots for £120 and £150. A man had bought shop plots for
> £300, and had sold them off at £700.

As the owner of the Manor of Gimingham Lancaster, Lord Suffield
owned the foreshore. In that capacity he gave permission in 1910 to Sir
Edgar Speyer of Sea Marge, and his neighbour at Lawn Cottage, the
publisher Sir Frederick Macmillan, to build a groyne extending into the
water.[9] A description of Lord Suffield riding his horse along the beach at
Overstrand at much this time gives a little insight into the way in which
people thought of him:[10]

> Lord Suffield comes crunching along the beach on his big brown horse.
> 'I believe he's always scheming to lay his place out.' Now, Sylvia and
> I are firmly impressed with the idea that the Lord of Overstrand is
> much too fond of his lovely seaside property to harbour any such fell
> intentions and prefer to believe that he simply takes a paternal interest
> in the place.
>
> 'Capitally made up,' mutters Our Special Artist. 'Those grey
> knickerbockers, that grey felt wide-awake, that crimson tie, those heavy
> gaiters, are all part of the stage squire's attire.'

Lord Suffield owned the Manor of Overstrand. Among the small
estates comprising that manor was one known as Corner Cottage in
Pauls Lane, Overstrand (see Chapter 12). This at one time extended to
over two acres. This estate was enfranchised in 1901. It was eventually
sold off in lots in 1955–57. The last remnant of this small estate to be
sold is known today as The Old Stable. On the deed of enfranchisement,
which the author possesses, is information going back to 1881 which

shows that it was mortgaged and that William Charles Mills was Lord Suffield's trustee.

Mills was Conservative member of parliament for Maidstone and a director of the merchant bank Glyn, Mills & Co., He married Lord Suffield's daughter, Alice in 1886. Lord Suffield gave them Hillingdon Park as a wedding present.

In 1898 Mills inherited the title of Baron Hillingdon. In the same year Lord Hillingdon commissioned Edwin Lutyens to design Overstrand Hall. Work began in 1899 and it was completed by 1901. Building stone is largely absent in Norfolk, but the county is rich in flints and clay. Lutyens was therefore designing and building in local materials he had not encountered before. Overstrand Hall is of architectural importance as the earliest example of any importance of Edwin Lutyen's vernacular work outside the Home Counties.

> It is apparent, when looking at Overstrand Hall, that it is a house produced by an architect still experimenting with ideas concerning style, construction, materials and organisation, but it shows Lutyens gaining confidence and a greater simplicity which had been absent from most of his designs up to this point.

A regular visitor there was Princess Victoria, the fourth child of Edward, Prince of Wales, and Princess Alexandra. Lady Hillingdon was one of her two best friends. Lord Hillingdon taught her to play golf. The gardens of Overstrand Hall were extensive. Today they are the site of a small estate known as Hillingdon Park.

By the late nineteenth century golf was a popular and fashionable pursuit of the upper classes. The main instigator in the formation of The Royal Cromer Golf Club was the Liberal Member of Parliament Henry Broadhurst who lived at Trent Cottage, then Overstrand, now Cromer. He recorded, His Royal Highness, [Edward, Prince of Wales] in response to my invitation, consented to act as patron and gave the first prize, a handsome silver bowl.[11] At a meeting held in the Vicarage Room, Cromer, on 30th January, 1888, for the purpose of confirming the rules, electing officers, and for other business. Mr. H.G. Winter presided. The Club was constituted as follows: Patron, H.R.H. the Prince of Wales; President, the Right Hon. Lord Suffield; Vice-Presidents, the Earl of Rosebery, B. Bond-Cabbell, Esq. (Chairman of the Committee), S. Hoare, Esq., M.P., J.J.

Colman, Esq., M.P., H. Broadhurst, Esq., M.P., Cyril Flower, Esq., M.P., S. Gurney Buxton, Esq., H.A. Barclay, Esq., and Geoffrey F. Buxton, Esq. The Reverend Henry C. Rogers of Wood Norton Rectory, East Dereham, was appointed Captain.

The Royal Cromer Golf Club was built on land largely owned by Lord Suffield:

> … the land now occupied by the golf links was nothing but a sand hill used for pasture, and not very good for that, bringing in only about eighty pounds a year. I turned it into a links, and immediately an effort was made to show that it did not belong to me at all. But we went to law about it, and proved it to be included in the Overstrand property bought for a large sum by my grandfather. Now it brings in £400 a year.[12]

Those on a golfing holiday needed a comfortable and convenient hotel in which to stay. In Cromer, Lord Suffield was partly responsible for the Royal Links Hotel: *I helped, too, to build the Links Hotel, an expensive affair, for there was nothing but a sand hill to build on, and very deep excavations had to be made for the foundations.* The hotel was formally opened at a garden party held in the grounds attended by, among others, Lord Suffield and Lady Hastings. The course had recently been extended from nine holes to eighteen and in the course of the afternoon Lady Hastings declared them open. A thirty-six hole exhibition match was subsequently played between the winner and runner-up in the Open Golf Championship. The grounds of the hotel extended to seven acres, including stabling for fifteen horses. Among the amenities the hotel offered were a comfortable entrance lounge and a drawing, coffee, reading and billiard room.

It will be seen from the above that the influence of Charles, 5th Baron Suffield, in the area known as Poppyland was extensive, covering access to the area, housing development, and the providing of amenities, including a plot for the Roman Catholic church. However, the motives behind his involvement were probably influenced more by the changed circumstances in the conditions of the landed classes than by the direct influence of Poppyland, whose influence it is difficult to assess. The following chapter covers part of the same ground as this chapter, but from the very different perspective of the changing circumstances influenced more directly by Poppyland.

The Royal Links Hotel on the top of the hill, with the lighthouse on the left. At the bottom of Happy Valley is the golf club house and in front of it the then first hole of the course.

1   Gunton papers in the Norfolk Record Office, GTN 3/2/1/3.
2   Charles Harbord, 5th Baron Suffield, *My Memories, 1830–1913* (London: Herbert Jenkins, 1913), p. 91.
3   Constance Battersea, *Reminiscences* (London: Macmillan, 1922), p. 345.
4   Lionel Cust, *King Edward VII and His Court* (London: John Murray, 1930), p. 153.
5   Gunton papers in the Norfolk Record Office, GTN 350/106/711X2.
6   *Eastern Daily Press*, 10th February 2007, p. 11.
7   Suffield, p. 84.
8   Gunton papers in the Norfolk Record Office, GTN 3/1/14/8.
9   I am grateful to Mr. G. Kidd for this information.
10   Annie Berlyn (Mrs. Alfred Berlyn), *Vera in Poppyland* (London: Jarrold, 1891), pp. 34–35.
11   Henry Broadhurst, *Henry Broadhurst, M.P.: The story of his life from a stonemason's bench to the Treasury bench* (London: Hutchinson, 1901), p. 156.
12   Suffield, p. 84.

7

The Flowering of Poppyland

The 1890s were not so much the ending of a century as the beginning of a new one.[1] The Cromer of the 1890s resembled the Cromer of the first decade of the twentieth century far more than it did that of the 1880s. Dr. Dent, who arrived in Cromer 1889, later commented:

> In 1889 Cromer did not aspire to any position above the dignity of fishing village. It was quite extraordinary to witness during the next ten years especially, its rapid development and ever-increasing popularity.

The population of Cromer during the decade between 1881 and 1891, increased by 642. In the following decade it increased by a massive 1,542. A similar pattern was repeated in Sheringham. The population doubled between 1891 and 1901, mainly affecting Lower Sheringham which developed into a town.

This situation was paralleled in Overstrand. When Cyril and Constance Flower bought their *Cottage* in Overstrand in 1888,

> ... this corner of Norfolk round Cromer had been chiefly owned by people of Quaker origin, often notable for their public spirit and philanthropy, Buxtons, Gurneys, Barclays and Hoares and their various offspring. There they lived quiet country lives.[2]

Ten years later Lady Battersea wrote in her journal:

> Overstrand is grown into a large and tiresome place. Lewises and Alexanders are going to build, and a big hotel will be close to us. No longer country. I cannot say I am pleased, but our garden is large and pretty and in every way it satisfies Cyril — the great thing .

The rapid development and growth may be seen in four areas: the growth of railways; the building of private housing; the building of luxury hotels and providing greater public amenities.

The railways contributed significantly to the explosion of popular holidays and the flowering of Poppyland. In 1887 Cromer was reached by railway from the west when the Eastern and Midlands Railway opened its extension from Holt to Cromer Beach station. The Eastern and Midlands Railway was a small railway that came into existence in 1882-3 after the amalgamation of several still smaller companies.

The company was ever short of money. The Midland Railway Company never gave the Eastern and Midlands any custom, but it was known to be seeking to expand its passenger traffic. The best hope for the Eastern and Midlands was to open a line to the holiday resort of Cromer, creating a direct rail link with the Great Northern Railway at Peterborough and beyond to the industrial cities of the Midlands via Stamford, in the hope of enticing the Midland to purchase.

Work began with a gang digging the Weybourne-Kelling cutting. Contracts for infrastructure for the line in the form of stations and bridges were given to local firms. Other railway work was carried out internally at the company's works at Melton Constable. Four new engines were ordered and two sets of second hand passenger carriages were purchased from the North London Railway. The Eastern and Midlands Railway terminus of the Holt branch was the present Cromer Beach station. The site of the *station was a small farm, house and buildings, also a spring pit 'Sheep's Hole'.*[3] The station boasted a fine new refreshment room three minutes walk from the cliff top and Jetty, as its name implies. The line to Cromer was opened on 17th June, 1887, in time for the summer traffic. Reporting on the Eastern and Midlands Railway's arrival at Cromer, the pictorial magazine *Illustrations* eulogised:

> A word now as to delightful Cromer, whose reputation has been rapidly increasing. People wishing for a quiet, bracing, healthy, and beautiful seaside resort are asked, 'Have you been to Cromer?' The answer being in the negative, there ensues the noting of the place as one to be visited at the very first opportunity.

A Kings Cross−Cromer service was the first through route to be inaugurated during the time of the Eastern and Midlands railway with three trains in each direction, which increased to five by 1889.

The Eastern and Midlands Railway was formally taken over by the

Midland and Great Northern Joint Railway on 1st July, 1893. On May 1st, 1894, a twenty mile extension from the Midland Railway at Saxby to Bourne was opened for passenger traffic,[4] creating a more direct route from the great Midland cities to the Norfolk coast. The importance of this direct route cannot be emphasised enough in the growth of Poppyland. It put an end to a detour that entailed an immense amount of trouble and loss of time. The daily *Leicester* quickly became the line's most prestigious express service. In July two eastbound trains used the new link with a through service between Birmingham and Great Yarmouth, usually with coaches to Norwich and Cromer. Excursion trains from the Midlands to the Norfolk coast were also run by Thomas Cook. The Midland and Great Northern Joint Railway developed through services to and from the Midlands and the north west. It was possible to book a ticket at Liverpool for Cromer and travel all the way in a coach with that name on the destination board.

The Kings Cross-Cromer service posed a serious threat to the Great Eastern Railway which till then had a monopoly of rail travel to the north Norfolk coast. Although the journey from Kings Cross took longer than that by the Great Eastern Railway from Liverpool Street, this was mitigated by the fact that the terminus at Kings Cross was closer to the more affluent parts of London than Liverpool Street, which also suffered from its association with the 'East End'. Once the traveller had arrived at Cromer Beach it was only a short walk to the various hotels to which luggage could be carried by hired porters.

On 3rd November, 1895, the Great Eastern Railway ran a trial non-stop train from Liverpool Street to Cromer in a time of two hours fifty-five minutes. On arrival the engine was found to be short of water. In July, 1897, following the installation of water troughs, the Great Eastern Railway introduced the *Cromer Express* running non-stop to North Walsham. There were no restaurant cars, but food baskets and hampers were available at a price, other passengers taking bottles of ale and sandwiches.

In 1907 the Great Eastern Railway introduced the 'Norfolk Coast Express'. This train consisted of new all-corridor coaches which in the summer months ran north-stop to North Walsham in a time of 158 minutes and to Cromer in 175 minutes. This train had through coaches for Mundesley and Sheringham. On the busiest days in summer the

Cromer carriages ran as a separate train. The railway had arrived in Mundesley in 1899 and a connection from Mundesley to Cromer was opened in 1906. In 1906 a connection was made between the Great Eastern Railway at Cromer and the Midland and Great Northern Joint Railway at Sheringham. *A former stationmaster has recalled as many as sixty-four trains a day steaming in and out of Sheringham station, many of them with special wagons to bring carriages, landaus and horses which accompanied those coming to stay in the town.*[5]

Poppyland, Cromer and Sheringham were now within easy travelling distance of millions from London, the south and the cities of the Midlands and the north. The railways afforded an incentive to local landowners to exploit their land for building. *The eye of the speculative builder is firmly fixed upon poor little Cromer,* commented Clement Scott, as he stood at Cromer railway station and looked down upon the little town, across an open expanse of fields.

In 1885 an historic sale of land from the Cromer Hall estate took place. The London firm of Baker and Sons auctioned 60 building plots, described as *sound and improving investments.* On 17th June a special train from London brought 200 investors, who lunched at the Hotel de Paris, before inspecting the plots and returning to the hotel for the auction. *Buyers were assured they would be taking part in a high class development.* This sale included plots on both the eastern and western boundaries of Cromer. On the eastern boundary St. Margaret's Terrace was built in the Norwich Road, stretching as far as the present Vicarage Road. The remainder of the development was on the western side of the town. The sale brochure stipulated *houses to be built on the two new roads, Prince of Wales Road and Hamilton Road, must not cost less than £450.*

Further successful auctions of land from the Cromer Hall estate took place in 1890 and 1891, with special trains from London and the Midlands bringing in prospective buyers. The prospectus for the 1890 sale is of particular interest as it refers to *Poppyland and the Garden of Sleep* as desirable reasons for purchase:

> ... *magnificently placed in the best part of Cromer, one of the healthiest seaside resorts on the east coast, and renowned for its long stretch of some of the finest sands in England, charmingly situated on the summit of a bold cliff, commanding grand sea and land views, embracing the lighthouses hill and Overstrand, the scene of Clement*

Scott's 'Poppyland and Garden of Sleep', affording the finest sites in Cromer for the erection of private marine residences and shops, the whole offering lucrative investments to builders and others.[6]

New roads were planned in a rectangular or grid pattern on the western side of the town. Many of the new houses became boarding houses or guest houses. In the late 19th century some skilled workers began to have paid holidays. They often went to stay at the seaside.
Benjamin Bond-Cabbell died suddenly in 1892.

Cromer in Mourning

A solemn gloom has fallen upon Cromer just at the commencement of the season, consequent upon the lamented death of Mr. Benjamin B. Bond-Cabbell, of Cromer Hall, to whom the development and prosperity of the town are so greatly due. By throwing building land into the market he has greatly assisted in the extension of the town.[7]

Further development took place on Cromer's eastern side. In 1893 Sir Samuel Hoare began the work of developing Cliff Avenue, which

The town of Cromer, as depicted on the brochure of the sale of land from the Cromer Hall estate, 1890.

had previously been pasture. Cliff Avenue runs parallel to the Norwich Road on its eastern side from the Overstrand Road, before linking up again with the Norwich Road. It was completed between 1893 and 1905. Fine individual residences were built in the Queen Anne style to attract wealthy clients. Many were designed by the Cromer architect, William Augustus Scott. Among the first residents was Dr. Dent who lived in Yerbury. In the late 1890s, as building progressed, Sir Samuel Hoare left Cliff House and moved to Sidestrand Hall, which the family had purchased in 1836.

At the beginning of the twentieth century a large portion of the centre of Overstrand bounded to the south by a proposed road following the route of the present Mundesley Road, then a track, from the present village sign to the junction with present Coast Road and to the north by the road that ran through the village, was offered for sale in lots. It was part of a larger area that had been bought by John Henry Gurney, M.P. for £6,000 in 1855. The undated brochure includes a few concise and well chosen words that reflect the essence of Poppyland at the acme of its fame and influence. The *General Description* extols the beauty of the area with its *ozone laden breeze* coming straight across the North Sea. The *Stipulations as to Building and Use* laid down a number of provisions to preserve the *select character* of the area. No plot of land was to be less than one half acre in size; individual houses must be built of the finest materials and cost not less than £600 each, excluding stables; no commercial development or use of any sort was permitted. The area is still devoid of shops.

The accompanying map to this brochure records the names of all the properties on the seaward side of the road, including properties beyond the Overstrand Hotel which have long disappeared owing to cliff erosion. These include The Croft, Poppy House and Danecourt. While The Gables is mentioned, the building that later became Sea Marge is merely called Villa.

There were both differences and similarities from Cromer in the development of Sheringham as a holiday resort. During much of the nineteenth century Cromer had been a select watering resort, while Lower Sheringham had been an insular fishing village, resenting intruders. Travel guides spoke of the charm and interest Cromer fishermen added to the local scene, whereas *the fishermen of Sheringham* had gained a reputation for being wild and reckless. They were given the nickname Shannocks (shanny is an archaic word from East Anglia meaning wild and foolish).[8] Conditions began to change in the early 1880s when there was a collapse in farming resulting in some of the poorer farm land in lower Sheringham being sold for development. Sheringham was expanding, but sanitation remained primitive, one earth closet served several cottages, the contents being dumped on the beach.[9] There had been an outbreak of typhoid fever in Sheringham in 1885 which resulted in the death of two visitors.

By the time the Eastern and Midlands Railway reached the town in 1887 the building boom was in progress. However, although Cromer was less than five miles away, there were people living in Sheringham who had never seen a locomotive. Mr. R.H. Upcher of Sheringham Hall was regarded as a kind of patriarch among his people. Both he and T. Wyndham-Cremer of Beeston Hall were strenuously opposed to the coming of the railway, but both remained on friendly terms with William Marriott, the railway's chief engineer. The arrival of the railway gave a considerable boost to the growth of Sheringham as an important holiday town:

> The Directors set up the first building estate, laid the main drain, got hotel and gas works built, and gave the place its start in life. Now its rivals Cromer in public appreciation, though there should be no rivalry between the two towns.[10]

In 1888 a description of Sheringham was published to coincide with the arrival of the Eastern and Midlands Railway. Historically this article is important as it portrays a snapshot of Sheringham at the very moment of its explosion into a seaside town. The opening paragraph paints the scene:

> A railway journey of five and a-half hours from Kings Cross carries the traveller to Lower Sherringham, [sic] a small fishing village on the north-east coast of Norfolk, having a newly-opened station on the Eastern and Midlands Railway. As yet, the Vandalic hand of the London builder has not been laid upon Sherringham; [sic] and the race of lodging-house keepers, of whom sundry trips to better known places render the British traveller very wary, has not been developed there, so it is still a pleasant place for an autumn holiday. We will walk down to

Sherringham beach - such as nature and the fishermen have made it - by the rough pathway which has sufficed for generations of villagers.[11]

As with so many travel writers, the local fishermen immediately grasped their attention.

The chief study on the beach is the fishermen themselves - a tall, handsome race of men, of splendid physique. Dressed in rich brown coloured jackets or bright yellow oilskins, huge boots reaching half way up the thighs, and sou'wester hats worn back to the front of the head when the sun is bright, with most beautiful effect - they are the very beau-ideal of their laborious class. The women go about with gay-coloured handkerchiefs on their heads, and some have quite Southern type beauty; indeed, I have seen some whom contadine of Italy could not rival.

Once on the beach, the correspondents were asked by an old fishermen whether they liked bathing.

'Oh, yes,' we replied.
'Well, never you bathe without a boat near. I goes out in my boat when people is bathing, and I keep about for just nothin' at all - sixpence each.' Then he explained how he erected tents for bathing, consisting of an old sail wrapped round four oars, stuck in the pebbles, one of which might be had for half a-crown a week.

At this time the cliff top overlooking the beach was largely occupied by fishermen's cottages.

Some of the people let rooms, and, of course, the visitor virtually lives in their cottages. These are built of stones taken from the beach and, though very small, are clean and comfortable. The style of architecture is borrowed from a ship's cabin; the windows in some are like port-holes; lockers are placed in convenient positions, and our staircase bore the strongest resemblance to a companion-ladder.

This contemporary reference to the letting of cottages in 1888 is historically important. Lady Battersea also recorded the same habits of the fishermen at Overstrand in the ten week summer season, but it must be remembered she was writing many years later.

In one respect, however, the development of Sheringham resembled

Fishermen's cottages in Sheringham, as depicted in a drawing of 1888.

that already seen at Cromer. The Upcher family had been lords of the manor and principal landowners in Sheringham since 1812 when Abbot Upcher bought the Sheringham estate. His son, Henry Ramey, opposed the coming of the railway, as has been noted above, and did little to encourage the development apart from providing land for a cliff-top golf course. However, Henry Ramey Upcher died on 30th March, 1892. His son, Henry Morris Upcher, inherited the estate and adopted a more progressive attitude. He laid out a building estate on the western edge of Sheringham fronting the Cromer Road which was sold off in portions in 1893, 1894 and 1897. It was described as undoubtedly occupying the finest position in Sheringham.

Further evidence of the impact of the coming of the railway upon Sheringham and Poppyland may be seen in a guide book of a slightly later date.[12] The author imagines that he has been asked by a London family to find them a suitably quiet seaside resort offering golf and a safe beach for the children. He visits Sheringham:

> ... time was when this was an old-world, sleepy fishing village, without railway, and with never a summer visitor. But one day there appeared on the bookstalls a little book called Poppy-land, and in the music shops a song entitled 'The Garden of Sleep', and then farewell to the

old-world Cromer and its little neighbour Sheringham.

He interviewed the landladies in the *highways and byways of Sheringham.* Finding it thirsty work, fate led him to the Lobster Inn.

This particular inn is not 'advanced.' There is no 'table d'hote' open to non-residents, but there is a kind host and hostess to give an old fashioned welcome. At the end of the passage one got a glimpse of the bar, where picturesque fisherman were quaffing Yarmouth ale.

He was invited to lunch with a Cambridge undergraduate who spent his weekends at the Lobster because he said he had *never met lobsters so perfectly cooked as at this identical inn.* As a result of his conversation, the author concluded *I feel I can quite confidently recommend my friend to go to Sheringham.* No doubt the friend and his family would have arrived by train.

Sheringham may have been a slow starter in the holiday trade, but it had caught up by the beginning of the twentieth century.

I would have you share my joy in the strip of Norfolk coast on what has hitherto been called the wrong side of Cromer. Time has before now turned a wrong into a right. Sheringham, the friendly rival of Overstrand, is bent on proving there is no wrong side of Cromer at all. Go to Sheringham, then, and the number of things you need not do will keep you happy all through the holidays. Seascape and landscape tug at the poor visitor until he is wearied by their rival claims upon him.[13]

The increase in housing development was matched throughout the area with an increase in the provision of hotel accommodation. In Cromer town centre the Red Lion Hotel was rebuilt in 1887. The Bath House hotel on the promenade was under new management in 1890 and underwent thorough repairs and renovation. The Hotel de Paris was re-built in 1894. The previous year saw the erection of the Metropole Hotel adjacent to Tucker's Hotel.

In 1906 the Metropole was described as the best hotel in Cromer, having been refurbished and provided with electric light. Several new large hotels were erected on the west side of Cromer following the three land sales. It is these larger hotels that have captured the imagination and helped to define the area. In Prince of Wales Road, on the corner of New Street, where now stands Morrison's petrol station, stood the imposing Marlborough Hotel, with its Moorish dome at the centre surrounded by elaborate gables. At the other end of the Road, on the corner of Hamilton Road, stood the Eversley Hotel, built 1902–3. In 1910 this hotel was advertising garages for residents. In 1902 Cromer had

The Grand Hotel at Cromer, built as the key development on the west cliff and described by a member of the staff of Punch *magazine as 'semi-grand'.*

been chosen as the destination for the Easter Tour of the Automobile Club.[14]

Further hotels were opened along the Runton Road facing the sea. The Grand Hotel was opened on 15th July, 1891. It was designed by the Norwich architect George Skipper and described in the local press as a handsome edifice in red brick with stone dressings. To celebrate its opening a banquet was held, presided over by Sir William Kemp, Bart., chairman of the company behind the hotel, whose home was The Close, now Glendon House, Overstrand. Sir Alfred Haslam, Mayor of Derby, accompanied by Lady Haslam, proposed a toast to the 'Success of the Grand Hotel'. During the course of his speech he said he had visited Cromer five years previously and had been advised it was necessary to secure accommodation a month in advance, proving the necessity for the hotel. He added *the impression gained from a visit to that lovely place on a bright July morning was one which could never be removed from his memory.*

This was followed in 1894 by the Cliftonville Hotel. The Sheringham Hotel, Sheringham, opened in 1889 just one hundred yards from Sheringham railway station and three hundred yards from the beach, on a most desirable situation on the slope of a hill. It contained thirty bedrooms and a large number of private apartments. The Grand Hotel, now demolished, opened in Sheringham in 1898. The Burlington Hotel was never completed owing to the development company going bankrupt, though the finished element did operae as a hotel until 2016.. Mundesley had a good selection of hotels, including the Clarence, Grand, Royal, Manor and Bitterlich's.

Over the 1890s, Overstrand's reputation as *a quiet watering place populated with a wide section of distinctly superior people,*[15] led to a high demand for accommodation. Suddenly Overstrand had become a fashionable place to be seen, where one could find a broad circle of people from upper class and aristocratic families, who were intellectually and in matters of taste, at the forefront of society.

Overstrand had little forewarning of the number of visitors which it would be expected to provide accommodation for over the busy summer period and so the wealthy had to make do with scant accommodation available. In 1899, plans for a hotel were made, to provide the upper classes with high quality accommodation.[16] The Overstrand Hotel was built on the cliff top in Overstrand Main Road, 1899-1900. The architects were the well known Norwich firm of Edward Boardman and Son. This firm tended to use *sober, classically inspired forms.* The hotel was provided with 57 bedrooms, stables and carriage washing yard.[17] By 1903 it had gained a reputation as being *one of the finest on the east coast.*[18] The hotel had a broad and impressive staircase. Upstairs the large bedrooms on the non-view south side were provided with shared bathroom and water closet facilities. *By this we realise that a view was more highly prized than the warmth of the sun.*[19] The Overstrand Hotel was noted for its fine brickwork. This applied particularly to the construction of the entrance porch by the Trimingham craftsman and brick layer, Thomas Kidd. In 1926 he founded a building firm still trading today under the name of E.C. Kidd. It is now run by Thomas's grandson, Michael, forming a continuous link with the past. Geoffrey Kidd is another grandson, to whom I am indebted for this information.

Mention must also be made of the White Horse Hotel in Overstrand,

The Overstrand Hotel, built 1899–1900. It was gutted by fire in 1949 and demolished in 1951.

which featured on Faden's map of Norfolk, 1794. Who knows who may not have stayed there at the height of Poppyland's fame?

The leisured classes who came to visit Poppyland needed a form of recreation. Golf was becoming popular. The Royal Cromer Golf Club was formed under the initiative of the Liberal Member of Parliament, Henry Broadhurst (see previous chapter).

The Sheringham Golf Club was formed in 1891. The course was laid out by the celebrated Tom Dunn. The original nine holes were increased to eighteen. The course is particularly favoured by lady golfers. When the Ladies' Golf Championship was held there, Fred Stibbons wrote: *I am privileged to witness this remarkable exhibition of the skill and prowess of my British sisters.*[20] The next golf club to open was that at Mundesley, which was established in 1901. It was designed by the six times open winner Harry Vardon and was beautifully situated on the rolling hillside of the River Mun. A golf course was opened at West Runton in 1903, following the building of an hotel by the local land owner James Abbs in 1899 and the provision of a railway station in 1892. The architect of the course was the professional John Henry Taylor, who is considered to be one of the pioneers of the modern game.

Not everyone was happy with the inexorable expansion of Cromer into a popular holiday resort. The opposition came from the old well-

Sheringham golf course, summer, 1906. Mr Ben Davies, the celebrated Welsh tenor, is about to drive. The Sheringham Hotel, opened 1889, with pointed domed corners, is visible towards the right background.

established families who had dominated the locality for the best part of the century. In 1887 John Gurney Barclay said in a speech that the proposal to build a new pier below the Red Lion Hotel would bring down upon them a large number of excursionists. Cromer for the past quarter of a century had had a constituency, so to speak, of its own — people belonging to the upper class, who came with their horses and carriages, and spent their money here, staying five or six weeks.

In 1888 at a public meeting to discuss the proposal to build a new town hall in Cromer, John Henry Buxton of Upton House commented, *visitors came to Cromer purely as being a place purely of the country, and not a Brighton or a Scarborough.*

The growth of Cromer into a holiday resort marked a waning in the influence the traditional landed families exercised upon the town. The same situation may be seen at Sheringham, but it was the fishermen who saw their traditional influence waning. The particular issue was the introduction of street lighting when the fishermen were outvoted by newcomers who wanted to improve their town. *The fishermen had to realise that their control of the community was rapidly slipping from their grasp.*[21]

An anonymous writer from Brighton was more scathing about the effects of development:

Poppyland — As It Was and Is.

Overstrand is the centre of the district which Cockney writers delight to call Poppyland. It has been very much overwritten of late years. I remember well as a boy before the railway went to Cromer or visitors had discovered it. Then it was one of the loveliest bits of coast anywhere in England. Its charm was its remoteness and quietness and in the unsophisticated manners of the villagers. You will look in vain for unsophisticated manners in Poppyland today. A few years' cultivation of the lodger crop has turned the villagers from simple peasants and fishermen into most adroit extractors of tips and fancy prices. The demoralisation that is painfully evident in most places where the pursuit of the lodger is the chief industry has nowhere gone further than in Poppyland. And as for rural charm and remoteness quietness, I would advise no one to go near Cromer for that nowadays. A fashionable lounger resort no doubt has its charms, but they are not the charms of simplicity and retirement.

An article in the *Morning Post* dated 19th September, 1890, draws attention to the changes wrought by Poppyland:

Mr. Clement Scott deplores the alterations which have taken place since he wrote about 'Poppy Land' and 'The Village on the Cliff'. Where some few years ago were only smiling cornfields, gay with scarlet poppies and here and there a labourer's cottage, are now red-brick villas and lodging houses. Perhaps he has himself to thank to some extent for having called attention to the beauties of his favourite resort. Still, those who visit the Norfolk coast will hear the reapers in the field, in accordance with a curious custom which must have come down from Norman times, demand 'largesse' from the passer-by in the phrase 'Please sta me a largesse, sir.' The advancing waves of summer visitors have swept away the majority of such old-time phrases.

The protests and adverse articles, however, did not put a stop to the development of Cromer. Over the centuries the foreshore and beach had sustained a constant battering from the sea and suffered much damage. By the end of the nineteenth century the old sea wall was in a parlous state. Between 1899 and 1901 it was replaced with the present fine sea wall, constructed entirely of concrete. The engineer was W.T. Douglass.

In 1897 the *Hero* struck Cromer jetty, damaging it beyond repair. The remains of the jetty were dismantled and sold by auction. Under the aegis of the Cromer Protection Commissioners a new pier was built. It was formally opened amid much enthusiasm on 8th June, 1901. The *Norfolk Chronicle* reported:

> Cromer — Queen of East Anglian watering places — on Saturday added another to its many attractions as a watering place — a new pier. Its natural charm of situation and its immediate vicinity to Poppyland have given Cromer a very large measure of popularity, although its distance from large centres of population has to some extent kept it more select than many of the other East Anglian resorts. By way of inaugurating the new pier the Great Eastern Railway conveyed a large party from London by special train on Saturday, and the journey of 140 miles was accomplished in the record time of two hours and forty-two minutes. Lord Claud Hamilton formally opened the pier in the presence of a large company, including Lord de Ramsey (Great Northern Railway), Mr. J.F.S. Gooday (Great Eastern Railway), and Mr. H. Broadhurst, M.P.

The Midland and Great Northern Railway sent invitations to editors of many provincial newspapers to the opening, which was fully reported in national and provincial newspapers in London, throughout the Midlands and as far north as Glasgow.

New or larger churches for the spiritual welfare of an expanding population were needed. A new chancel for Cromer parish church was added in 1887–89. Further repairs were carried out to the tower, the roof of the nave and the side aisles were lengthened. The mission church of St. Martin was built in Mill Road for the population of Suffield Park, 1897–8. The Wesleyan chapel mentioned in a previous chapter was replaced by a larger Methodist church designed by Frederick Scott, who later designed the Baptist Church. On June 2nd, 1886, Clement Scott wrote to the Catholic Bishop of Northampton asking for the provision of a priest to celebrate Mass at Abbot's Hall, Aylsham, the home of Mrs. Shepherd, for the benefit of holiday makers. In 1894 the Bishop spoke of his intention to a build a Catholic church at Cromer. Lord Suffield leased him an acre of land then situated in the parish of Overstrand adjacent to the golf club. The blessing and opening of the new church took place on

25th August, 1895. A resident priest was appointed in 1902. *The bounds of the newly formed parish were reputed to have extended on the coast from Weybourne to Horsey Mere and said to have included the towns of North Walsham, Sheringham, Aylsham and Holt.* The historic catholic parish of north Norfolk was reduced in status to a Mass centre in 2010.

In Sheringham St. Peter's Anglican church replaced the old mission church in 1897. Sheringham had its fair share of Methodist Churches, including Primitive Methodists, 1844, and Free Methodists, later called the United Methodist Church. The Salvation Army opened a hall in Cremer Street in 1897. St. Joseph's Catholic Church was dedicated in 1910.

In Overstrand the ruined, ivy clad ancient parish church was restored and dedicated on the eve of Whitsunday, 1914, by the Bishop of Norwich. The smaller Christ Church, which had been built in 1867, was demolished in 1951.

It was fashionable to spend a holiday in Poppyland. The names of visitors were given to post offices and subsequently printed in the local newspapers. In June, 1890, at least three hundred holiday makers were staying in Cromer and a further thirty in Overstrand. It is indicative of the national interest in Cromer as a holiday centre that the following piece occurred in the *Aberdeen Telegraph* in August, 1898:

> *Miss Fanny Davenport, the American actress is now in England, but like Nat Goodwin, who is here again, she has no intention of appearing in public. Miss Davenport, who is making a purely non-professional tour, was last week in Cromer, where Mr. and Mrs. Fred Terry — described in the visitor's book as Edward Terry — are spending their holiday. Mr. Clement Scott, who comes and goes, has made more than one flying visit to these parts before departing to Wiesbaden, where the critic of the Daily Telegraph hopes to repair a nervous system that has been somewhat shaken by thousands of nights at the play. Mr. and Mrs. B.L. Farjeon are at Cromer with their family.*

Benjamin Farjeon had a remarkable life story. Born in poverty in the east end of London, he emigrated to Australia, moving on to New Zealand. His writing attracted the attention of Charles Dickens and he returned to England in 1868, living in the Adelphi Theatre. Over the next thirty-five years he produced nearly sixty novels.

In 1896 he brought his wife and four gifted children to spend a holiday with farmer Abbs at Manor Farm, East Runton. The sense of freedom, fun and adventure pervades descriptions of this holiday. This can be understood better when contrasted with the life in London they had just left: *hansoms, horse-buses, governesses, tutors and schools.*

The main occupation of the Farjeon children was cricket. At East Runton they played in a narrow field adjacent to Manor Farm in which the seeds were sown for their love of the game in later life. The Farjeons spent the last three summers of the nineteenth century at The Grange, Trimingham. Here again cricket was very much on the agenda. They played in a meadow, on the beach and when the weather was inclement in out buildings or even in a bedroom corridor, with a tennis ball, hair brush for a bat and a chamber pot for stumps.

During this holiday the family encountered Louie Jermy for the first time.

> I remember one moment of Louie, however, on that first visit – a moment when she was standing in a queerly papered bedroom, and telling us how, when she was a little girl, she papered the room herself.

These holidays generated lasting and deep memories:

> But perhaps the strangest thing about memories is that they are so peculiarly our own. There is a gate in Trimingham – I swung on it as a small boy – that signifies to me all the glories of conquest. To others it may be just a gate, or a squeak. And there are people among my Norfolk memories whose significance to me bears little or no relation to their significance to other folk, or even to themselves. There were picnics in fairy woods, and adventures in oceans of green bracken taller than ourselves. We rode stubborn donkeys, struggling to get them to start, and then struggling even more earnestly to get them to stop. Life was packed with thrills and drama.[22]

Twenty years later J. Jefferson Farjeon was still visiting Louie Jermy when the Mill House was so full she put him up on a sofa in her parlour: *yes, of course, I'll put you up here, if there's nowhere else to go.*

In these days of mass travel and package holidays, it is difficult to comprehend the excitement to such families a holiday to the seaside generated. Arrival at the station itself was exciting:

Cromer station was — and still is — one of the loveliest conclusions to a railway journey in the whole of England. You step out of the train and gaze down upon a pleasant, well-foliaged slope to the roofs of the picturesque little town, and beyond is the sparkling blue sea. Surely no sea horizon could really be as high as this! [23]

The atmosphere was one of bustle and excitement.:

There is a shrill crowd of excited females fighting for luggage on the platform, and small groups of children scrambling under everybody's feet, and doing their best to get crushed under barrow-loads of trunks and tents, and mail carts. [24]

On arrival at Cromer station children rushed down to the beach, while the adults followed in a horse bus. This itself left a vivid impression. One recollection is of the smell of *straw and stuffiness*, while another remembers *the great treat was driving down in the horse buses*. Families would then go their individual ways, perhaps to meet up later.

The Mottram family from Norwich were holidaying in Overstrand at much the same time as the Farjeons were at East Runton. Ralph Mottram, 1881–1971, was the son of the Chief Clerk of Gurney's Bank in Norwich. He was brought up in Bank House on Bank Plain in Norwich. He became Lord Mayor of Norwich in 1953. Ralph Mottram described

Cromer station, where there was 'a shrill crowd of excited females, fighting for luggage'. Hopefully there was more decorum for the arrival of Princess Alexandra as seen in this picture from 1902.

the cottage the family stayed in when he was a boy:

> We always hired the comparatively modern part of Mrs. Roger's house
> in Overstrand. That is to say, she had a little old flint cottage of four
> incredibly tiny rooms, ill-lighted by casement windows, with a wooden
> stair mounting up from the rearward one on the ground floor, to that
> above, an earth privy outside, and all water fetched from a well on
> the other side of the street. Onto this, in Napoleonic times, had been
> built a stucco fronted churchwarden-gothic enlargement, which can be
> dated by the fact that, in the nineties, one of the upper bedrooms had
> a window bricked up and blinded by tar, on the outside, to dodge Mr.
> Pitt's window tax.[25]

In the 1891 census Mrs. Rogers is recorded as a seventy-seven year
old widow living with her grandson in the Londs. The above description
fits the cottage known today as Crab Cottage in The Londs. Mottram
remembered *the lovely light evenings, the gradual deepening of the blue of
the dusk, the quieting murmur of sea after sundown.* He didn't feel like bed.
He slipped out and went down the Londs, despite a warning from Mrs.
Rogers about *Ole Black Shuck Dawg.* Mottram continued his account:

> I hadn't gone very far before there was a rustling in the thick hedge.
> I must own I didn't like it. I began to wonder if after all I would not
> be more comfortable in bed, than out in this damp and eerie place. I
> didn't believe in dogs without heads of course! But there, again, was
> the rustling. I made a vigorous effort, worthy of my mother, stumbled
> through the ditch, and thrust the tall stems to one side. There in the
> meadow beyond was a dark shape, four legged, and surely headless. My
> heart missed one beat. But not another, for the thing moved, and was
> clearly a placid old donkey that went in Larry Reynolds' 'governess'
> car.

The donkeys were kept in stables which were situated on the site
of the present Cliff Top Café. In the fullness of time the donkey died
and required a burial plot. Canon Carr, the Rector of Overstrand, was
approached to see whether it could be buried in the churchyard. He
decided on the whole it would not be appropriate. The donkey was
eventually buried in a field at the bottom of Tolls Hill, Overstrand. As it
was lowered into the grave the following was said:

Ashes to ashes,
Dust to dust.
If Canon Carr won't have you,
Tolls Hill must.[26]

A descendant of the Gurneys of Earlham through both her parents recorded her memories of holidays in Cromer before 1914:

> We spent most of our time on the beach; that was the only thing we wanted to do. I think we'd usually take our tea down. The first day you were there, you were allowed to take your shoes off, but you weren't allowed to paddle; the next day you could paddle; the next day after that you could bathe.[27]

The bathing costumes worn by women or girls consisted of long frocks with long elastic knickers underneath which filled with sand when the wearer sat on the beach. They were agony to pull down because the sand scraped the skin. Men wore all-in-one costumes in which the legs came down almost to the knees and with sleeves. Changing took place in bathing machines. These were a cause of great excitement as the prospective bathers tried to get in them before they were pulled into the sea by a horse, which could be fastened to back or front, depending on the state of the tide. The bathing machines went about two feet deep into the water. They were provided with ropes on the front on which to hang. It was 'the thing' to stay in the water as long as possible.

The bathing machines were either singles or doubles, and they had a most peculiar smell. The floor was always wet and sandy. They were very dark inside, because they only had little windows — and rather a crowd when there were several undressing at a time.

Tents were often employed for the purpose of changing. These could present difficulties.

> But to return to the tent. The Shadow insisted upon putting this up himself. He was sure he could do it unassisted, and scorned our suggestion of employing a fisherman to rear it for us. For a time we left him to himself, and watched from a distance his noble efforts to battle with the breeze, but as the wind was blowing from the sea, and as he was ultimately observed to be ascending, in the distended sail-cloth, the side of the cliff, we thought it time to go to his rescue.[28]

An official Great Eastern Railway postcard of east beach, Cromer, circa 1905. The bathing machines, with their steps into the sea, are drawn up at the water's edge. The GER crest is top right of the card.

But tents presented even greater hazards:

> An independent party, like ourselves, had erected their own tent apart from the rest, and with refreshing innocence had omitted to put a top on it. We heard muffled laughter proceeding from the Shadow and The Artist, when its owners had disappeared within it after their matutinal dip, and presently Sylvia and I found that our unsuspecting young friends were treating the amused spectators to a shadow pantomime, for the sun having filled the roofless tent with light, the outlines of the occupants were of course distinctly visible on the sheeting from without.[29]

In 1888 a family from London consisting of father and mother, an eighteen year old girl, three younger brothers and a friend spent a holiday in Sheringham. The family bussed to St. Pancras Station where they caught a crowded train. After a tortuous journey they finally arrived at Sheringham at 9 p.m. on a wet evening. The father had to return to London after a few days, but the remainder stayed nearly six weeks. Their house was situated on the cliff top. They found their cook more willing to talk about local traditions than the less communicative fishermen. The diary kept by the elder daughter provides an insight into the coastal or inland picnics and games. They visited local beauty spots. They thought Pretty Corner was a disappointment and Roman Camp a fraud, but they enjoyed paddling in the muddy bog on Beeston Common and picking wild flowers. They attended worship at the Chapel of Ease. Much of the service they found to be comic and the matter of fact way in which the old man playing the harmonium said 'Amen' nearly made them explode with laughter. They were impressed with aspects of the Salvation Army service. However, it was rather spoiled for the young diarist by the way in which the Captain sang the hymn *We Shall Have a Mansion There* in the style of a music hall song.

Once again the Lobster Inn figures prominently in a visitor's description of life in Sheringham at this time.

> *We went to the entertainment at the Lobster Inn after supper, which was quite one of the most amusing I have ever been at. The fisherman's band played to us frightfully out of tune, a fisherman sang for us, Mr. Grimes danced a hornpipe which was quite wonderful. The most amusing person there was Mr. Grimes, the way he danced 'Sir Roger' had us in fits. We danced to both the band's music and our own. I played the hornpipe and a lady played Waltzes. Mother and Aunt Alice crowned everything by dancing a polka to 'Pop Goes the Weasel'! All of us were there, and we enjoyed it furiously.*

In the days before the telephone was in general use, visitors to Poppyland needed a means to inform their families and friends of their safe arrival, the time of their home-coming and the state of the weather. Postcards were produced in their hundreds of thousands and are avidly collected today. Some are rarer than others and can fetch considerable sums of money on Ebay today. The terse and brief messages on the back provide an authentic insight into the social life of the time. The Great Eastern Railway produced sets of postcards, both in black and white and colour, illustrating East Anglian coastal resorts, including Cromer. These cards carry the railway's coat of arms, but they do not specifically refer to Poppyland

For visitors wishing to take home keep-sakes or presents, Goss type china was available depicting local scenes including the Garden of Sleep and the deserted Sidestrand church tower. Poppyland china, decorated with a design of poppies, buds and leaves was available. Jarrolds, Rounce and Wortley of Cromer, and B.A. Watts of Sheringham all sold Poppyland china to their own designs. A wide range of china was available, including whole tea or dinner services. The Royal Worcester china factory produced a jam pot depicting the Sidestrand church tower. A Cromer chemist produced 'Poppyland Bouquet', which at the time was sold world-wide.

1   Richard le Gallienne, in Franny Moyle, *Constance: the tragic and scandalous life of Mrs Oscar Wilde* (London: John Murray, 2011), p. 184.
2   Lucy Cohen, *Lady de Rothschild and her Daughters, 1821–1931* (London: John Murray, 1935), p. 220.
3   Alfred Collison Savin, *Cromer in the County of Norfolk: a modern history* (Holt: Rounce & Wortley, 1937), p. 135.
4   *Building a Railway: Bourne to Saxby* ed. Stewart Squires and Ken Hollamby (Woodbridge: Boydell Press for the Lincoln Record Society, 2009), p. 138.
5   Peter Brooks, *Sheringham: the story of a town* (Cromer: Poppyland Publishing, 1980; new ed. 2013), p. 18.
6   Cromer Hall estate sale brochure, 1890, in Cromeer Museum (CRRMU 1981.80.1678).
7   *Eastern Daily Press*, 25th May, 1892.
8   Peter Cox, *The Divided Village* (Sheringham: Courtyard Publishing, 2000), p. 25.
9   Peter Cox, *The Village Becomes a Town* (Sheringham: Courtyard Publishing, 2001), p. 6.
10   William Marriott, *Forty Years of a Norfolk Railway: Sheringham, Midland and Great Northern* (Midland & Great Northern Joint Railway Society Publications, 1974).
11   Francis G. Heath, *Illustrations* (W. Kent & Co., 1888), p. 34.
12   T. West Carnie, In *Quaint East Anglia* (Greening, 1899), p. 34.
13   *The Bystander*, 25th July 1906, pp. 177–178.
14   *The Motor-Car Journal*, 5th April, 1902.
15   *The Court Circular*, 25th April, 1903.
16   Frances Flower, *Overstrand, 'The Village of Millionaires': a study of architectural develop ents, 1888–1914* (University of St. Andrews, Department of Art History, Senior Honours Dissertation, 1993, in Cromer Museum), p. 27.
17   Christopher Pipe, *A Dictionary of Cromer and Overstrand History* (Cromer: Poppyland Publishing, 2010), pp. 148–149.
18   *The Court Circular*, 25th April, 1903.
19   Flower, p. 30.
20   In *the King's Country*, Frederick Stibbons, Henry Hartley, 1930, p. 117.
21   Cox, *Village Becomes a Town*, p. 25.
22   Herbert Farjeon, *Beyond the Bell*
23   Farjeon, p. 15.
24   Annie Berlyn (Mrs. Alfred Berlyn), *Vera in Poppyland* (London: Jarrold, 1891), p. 13.
25   Ralph Mottram, *Autobiography with a Difference* (London: Robert Hale, 1938), p. 72.
26   I am indebted to John Worthington for this memory.
27   Berlyn, p. 27.
28   Berlyn, p. 27

8

Lord and Lady Battersea at Overstrand

In 1877 Cyril Flower married Constance de Rothschild, daughter of the late Sir Anthony de Rothschild and his wife, Lady Louisa Rothschild. Both were born in 1843. Constance Rothschild was a daughter of one of the oldest and most prestigious merchant banking families in Europe. She was brought up in the Jewish faith of her ancestors in the comfortable surroundings of Aston Clinton, Buckinghamshire. Cyril Flower was the son of Philip William Flower of Furze Down Park, Surrey and Mary, daughter of Mr. J. Flower. Philip Flower had made a fortune as a wool merchant through trade with Australian connections. He was the founder of the firm of P.W. Flower & Company of Moorgate. He moved into property development and financed developments in Victoria Street, Pimlico and Battersea.

Cyril Flower was a bright boy, full of high spirits and fun. He was educated at Harrow and Trinity College, Cambridge graduating in 1867. Cyril is reputed to be the model for Eric in Canon Farrer's *Eric or Little by Little.* He was a man of great personal charm. A Cambridge contemporary wrote of him:

> The more I see of Flower, the more interesting he becomes as a psychological study. He is the only instance with which I am acquainted of a man whom the whole world has agreed, with one consent, to pet, from Whewell (Master of Trinity) to the white-aproned men who carry baked meats from the kitchens on their heads; nobody can resist him. Artists are perpetually painting him. In short, he is the irresistible man.[1]

Constance de Rothschild also found him irresistible. In 1864 he rode over from Mentmore with Constance's cousin, Leopold de Rothschild, to pay a visit. Constance records her impressions:

> I can remember that we were much struck by the good looks of Leo's friend; his fine features, bright dancing eyes, mass of waving golden hair and ruddy complexion produced a picture of youth, vigorous, health, and bright activity such as one seldom sees. He was bubbling over with fun and nonsense, and yet, at that early stage of his life, had the eye to notice and the knowledge to appreciate much of the artistic furniture in our house, so carefully selected by my father.[2]

Lord Battersea – an irresistible man.

At first sight Cyril and Constance seemed to have little in common. Constance de Rothschild had led a full life, busy with reading, writing, society and multifarious activities; and in many ways her tastes were dissimilar to those of her husband – Constance's sedentary, Cyril's active; hers philanthropic, his artistic.[3]

At this stage of their relationship, however, there was no question of marriage.

Cyril Flower entered the legal profession. He worked hard and his early career showed promise. In 1870 he was called to the bar. However, in 1872 his father died, when Cyril and his brothers inherited their family's business. Cyril did not find the work of developing property congenial. He took little direct interest in the day to day running of the firm and left much of the control in the hands of others. His interests lay elsewhere. Cyril Flower was a collector and patron of the arts. He was a close friend and patron of Edward Burne-Jones and one of the first to recognise his talent. In his collecting habits he had much in common with the aesthetes. He collected paintings by Botticelli and other early artists as well as Chinese blue and white porcelain. His houses were full of the beautiful objects collected, it would seem, out of a spontaneous love for them, rather than making a disciplined collection, as is the mark of the true collector.

In 1872 a crisis occurred in the family of Sir Anthony and Lady Louisa de Rothschild. *Cousin marriages were frequent among the Rothschilds.*[4] Constance's parents were first cousins. Lionel and Charlotte de Rothschild were hoping their son, Nathaniel, would marry one of his English cousins, Constance or Annie, daughters of Sir Anthony and Lady Louisa de Rothschild. It was not to be. Their younger daughter, Annie, had fallen in love with the Hon. Eliot Yorke, son of Lord and Lady Hardwicke of Wimpole Hall, Cambridgeshire, with whom the Rothschilds had been friendly for some time. Constance records in her journal in September that *the gentlemen had been out shooting.* The sisters met them and Annie and Eliot walked home together. After dinner that evening, Eliot spoke to Sir Anthony: *then came the scene. I shall never forget it,* wrote Constance.

The news came as a bombshell to Annie's parents. The situation was unprecedented. No member of the family had previously married outside their faith, nor was there any chance Annie was going to renounce the Jewish faith and no way Eliot would adopt Judaism. Anthony Rothschild had discussions with his brother, Joseph, and members of New Court, the City Offices of the House of Rothschild. *Papa came home in the evening quite against it. Eliot left. Annie was miserable.* The crisis continued into October. *We hardly eat or sleep and lead quite an excitable life. The feeling is weighing on me that a storm is brewing,* wrote Constance. She advised her sister to speak to her father and *force a consent from him. With her brave, courageous spirit, she actually went to Papa and had it out with him. He gave consent. Annie is allowed to write to Eliot. Joy!*

The marriage of the Hon. Eliot Yorke and Annie de Rothschild took place first in a Registry Office in the presence of some members of both families. Constance wrote on 11th February: *Annie's first wedding day. It was a most melancholy affair. Papa looked so sad and we all felt it so dreadfully.* A religious ceremony followed later in the private chapel at Wimpole Hall, Cambridgeshire. This was first time any member of the Rothschild family had married outside her own faith, without first entering her husband's community. It was also the first time that any English peer's son had become connected with a Jewish family, where the wife remained true to her own persuasion.

This marriage opened the way for Constance to marry Cyril Flower. They were married by Cyril's former Headmaster at Harrow, Canon Farrar, in November 1877. Following Lady Rothschild's bereavement the previous year, it was an understood condition that she should not be alone at Aston Clinton. Cyril Flower was a keen huntsman and the newly married pair spent the hunting season there. They made their London home at Surrey House on the corner of Edgware Road, opposite Marble Arch.

Lady Battersea recalled: *I can remember that shortly after our marriage Cyril told me how he hoped, one day, to go through the magic doors of the House of Commons as M.P.*[5] His ambition was known to a few close friends, including Lady Elizabeth Biddulph. It was her husband, Member of Parliament for Herefordshire, who suggested to Cyril that he fight the constituency of the Borough of Brecon, South Wales, at the next General Election.

Cyril Flower won the constituency in General Election of 1880, serving as its Member of Parliament for twelve years. In 1886 he was appointed Chief Whip. When the constituency of Brecon was prorogued, he was elected Member of Parliament for South Bedfordshire. In the administration of the Liberal Prime Minister, William Gladstone, Cyril served as a Junior Lord of the Treasury between February and July, 1886, when the party went into opposition.

For some years Cyril and Constance had been in the habit of taking a summer holiday at a hotel on the north Norfolk coast which Cyril found attractive. Cyril's mother came from Feltwell in south west Norfolk. Another attraction was their friendship with Lady Lothian at Blickling Hall. They had practically decided on buying a house in Sheringham when an epidemic of typhoid fever resulting in fatalities was declared close to their prospective purchase, causing them to change their minds. As has been recorded, they purchased two adjoining villas in the village of Overstrand, situated two miles east of Cromer. A description of this property is to be found in the brochure of Lord Suffield's auction of building plots in Overstrand in 1888 and may be of interest. At the time of the auction it was being leased to Cyril Flower. Lot 100 was described as:

The Desirable and Prettily-designed Freehold Semi-Detached Villa Residence fronting Harbord Road, Consisting of — on the Ground

Floor, Dining Room, Drawing Room, Breakfast Room, Kitchen, Scullery, Pantry, Larder, stores and outside offices: on the first floor — Five bedrooms; on the second floor Two bedrooms. Also stabling for two horses, Coach House, and Garden in rear.[6]

Lot 101 was described *as identical* to the above. It will be noticed the semi-detached villas were described as *fronting Harbord Road.* In the plan accompanying the 1888 auction Harbord Road was shown as running without deviation from south to north. Only the southern section of the road was ever built as planned, because Lord Battersea purchased the remaining land further north for his estate. The remainder of the present Harbord Road was to have been called Sea View Road.

Immediately Cyril became of something of a minor celebrity and a centre of interest to local inhabitants:

For Aunt Mahala, Mr. Cyril Flower's red cliff-side cottage, with its pretty verandah and its garden of poppies, has almost equal fascination, and her intense interest in the comings-in and goings-out of the Liberal Whip excites Our Special Artist to much ribaldry at her expense.[7]

It took Constance a little time to get used to her new house. She wrote in 1889: *August 30th, Cyril's birthday. Very cheery and happy, but, oh, this is an odious place, cold, draughty, windy, bitter, bleak, almost ugly — I dislike it heartily. Why did we ever come here?* Almost immediately Cyril began making improvements to the property. In August, 1891, Constance wrote:

Came down to my seaside home. Dear Cyril met me at the station with Fly-away in the cart. We came to our cottage - oh, what a transformation scene! I was simply astounded; I could not believe such a change possible. A large garden, a pretty drawing-room, a comfortable sitting-room, no draughts, no cold anywhere. We sat outside until a late hour.

However, with the passing of time it became clear that *The Cottage* was too small for the needs of Cyril and Constance, who wrote, *as it then stood, there were not sufficient rooms to house the guests whom Cyril loved to see about him, and the temporary additions that he had made proved, to say the least, most unsatisfactory.* The future course of events is best told in the words of Lady Battersea herself:

He was therefore very soon in his element, planning, altering, and rebuilding, and, as he was an adept in the art of picturesque construction, he found plenty of scope for his powers. Mr. Lutyens, now Sir Edwin Lutyens (the gifted young architect just then coming into public notice), entered fully into my husband's views; between them they evolved out of the old cottage a truly original, but certainly comfortable, home-y abode, which we renamed the Pleasaunce[8] at Lord Morley's suggestion.[9]

Two theories have been suggested for the choice of Edwin Lutyens as the architect. One is that it was partly on the recommendation of his cousins, the Wickham Flowers at Great Tangley.[10] Lutyens knew the house as Gertrude Jekyll, the celebrated gardener, had taken him there prospecting, but the architect was Philip Webb. The second suggestion is that Cyril and Constance entered the circle of Lutyens through sharing the same circle of friends as his wife and by the time of the Lutyens' marriage in 1897, the Batterseas can be regarded as intimate friends.[11]

No plans for the house exist and indeed may never have existed. The date of these various alterations is not known with certainty. However, it is known that the earth removed from the building was used to fill in the 'gap' in the cliffs,[12] which can be seen in old photographs. Work began to encase the original villas based on Lutyen's directions. Soon the villas were swarming with bricklayers and carpenters to encase them in Lutyen's design. It is impossible to know exactly what he designed, for there were almost daily alterations at first by Cyril, and then by Constance whose visits were less frequent. There is a tradition that when Constance surveyed a particular addition she did not like, she took it upon herself to demand the workmen to alter it, much to the chagrin of Edwin Lutyens when he reappeared. The long brick cloister recalls Webb's covered walk at Great Tangley. There is a village rumour that it may have been included to ensure greater privacy. Lutyens ultimately regarded his creation as a muddle. This is hardly surprising if credence can be placed upon E.F. Benson's comments:

> No one quite knew what happened to the villas; he himself [Cyril Flower] was puzzled about it. They were not pulled down, but ingeniously embedded, like flies in amber, in the structure which grew up round them. For years it was in a state of architectural flux.[13]

The house contains a number of points of interest. The door of the inner hall is Moroccan. It is inlaid with ebony, ivory and mother-

The Pleasaunce in the 1930s, showing its full extent and how the original villas were 'ingeniously embedded, like flies in amber, in the structure'.

of-pearl. The inscription over the door is in Arabic. The fireplace in the drawing room is surrounded by some fine arts and crafts tiles. The lamps on the stairway and landing are from a Venetian gondola. Lutyens designed many of the interior fittings. Lord and Lady Battersea were great travellers and collectors, filling the house with rare and interesting objects they brought home on their travels

With the general election in 1892, Cyril Flower had served twelve years in the House of Commons. These years were described as *one of usefulness to the party, rather than interference in debate.* Outside the House of Commons he had proved himself an excellent speaker travelling to all parts of the country. He gave notable service to his party by his social entertainments. His London house became a meeting place for members of all parties.

His interest in art naturally led to an interest in the national collections. It was through his intervention that Raphael's *Ansidei Madonna* and van Dyck's equestrian portrait of King Charles I were saved for the nation from the sale of paintings at Blenheim Palace in 1885 and are now in the National Gallery, London.

Following the Liberal victory in the 1892 general election, Cyril Flower was hoping for high office in the new government on completion of his term as chief whip. Constance was disappointed when her husband was offered a peerage.

> The peerage meant an end to the old Parliamentary life, so full of adventure, surprises, and incidents, and I felt inwardly that Cyril would never take the same position in the Lords that he had had in the House of Commons. Besides which, being a consistent radical, I hardly looked upon a peerage as promotion.

Cyril took the title of Baron Battersea of Battersea in the County of London and Overstrand in the County of Norfolk. His acceptance was an event of some adverse comment at the time.

> He thought he could remain as good a Radical when a Peer as when a Member, and with an odd defect of humour, quoted the lines, 'There is no office in this needful world but dignifies the doer if done well,' which would be more appropriate if he had accepted an Inspectorship of Sewage.[14]

On 1st February, 1893, Lady Battersea wrote: Cyril came home at 6.30, saying, I have good news for you. He flung himself into a chair and said, 'I have been offered the Governorship of New South Wales. It was in Sydney, New South Wales, that Cyril's father had begun his successful career. To have accepted the appointment would have been a glittering and fitting end to Lord Battersea's career. It struck me like a knife, Lady Battersea wrote. Knowing Cyril's devotion to her [Lady Rothschild] and his oft-expressed determination of never leaving her for long, I thought, foolishly indeed, that he would agree with me in the advisability of refusing the offer.

Deeply attached to her mother as she was, Lady Battersea could not contemplate leaving her for the other end of the world. But she was mistaken in her surmise. Cyril wished to accept the offer. Constance and Annie travelled to Aston Clinton to see Lady de Rothschild. In a walk after lunch they told her the news. It was a bolt from the blue.

Lord Battersea left the final decision to Lady de Rothschild and Constance. The decision was 'no'. On 6th February, Lady Battersea wrote in her journal, a letter sent to Lord Ripon. I added a few lines. Miserably weak: I do not feel fit for anything. She wrote: Cyril performed one of the greatest acts of renunciation, greater than ever my dear mother could ever have been aware of, for her sake and mine.

This decision had a profound effect upon the influence exercised by Lord and Lady Battersea upon Overstrand and Poppyland in the succeeding years. In order to understand it, it is necessary to appreciate the close attachment Constance had for her mother. In 1882 she wrote in her journal: *Fast Day. Spent it with dear Motherkins ... With her, sunshine; without her, cold shade. Her love transforms me, her delicacy refreshes me. God be praised at having given me such a Mother!* Lady Louisa de Rothschild was by any standards an exceptional woman. Although small of stature and frail of health, she was, nevertheless, a forceful character. Her principal interests were a deep concern for the welfare of the poor, education and religion. It has been suggested that she exercised as much influence over her daughters as Queen Victoria exercised over hers.

The decision to decline the Governorship of New South Wales was a turning point in the career of Lord Battersea. He was a disappointed man. He lost interest in politics and gave up the idea of public life. To the end of her life, Constance worried over her decision to thwart her husband's ambition. She wrote later in her *Reminiscences: Were I to live my life over again I think I should act differently, for, to say the least, it is ill-judged, perhaps unpardonable, to stand in the way of man's acceptance of an honourable and useful career.* For a time it cast a shadow in the relationship of Lord Battersea and his mother-in-law. In February, 1893, Lady de Rothschild wrote: *Cyril's disappointment and anger about the New South Wales appointment made me feel most uncomfortable. He was evidently disappointed in me, as I am in him!* Lady de Rothschild never fully realised the sacrifice Cyril had made on her behalf, nor did she show her appreciation. Thus it was that Lady Battersea's attachment to her mother, resulting in her refusal to go to Australia, ensured Cyril and Constance's continued presence at the Pleasaunce, which henceforth became their main country residence. Lord Battersea and Lady Battersea threw themselves into local life.

The influence they exerted through their direct involvement in the life of Overstrand is inestimable. Lord Battersea had an empathy with children and the elderly. He secretly carried fresh milk, fruit and cakes to a village youth dying of consumption. He devoted himself to beautifying the Pleasaunce. He acquired more land for a cricket pitch. He built the Reading Room, which was opened by Princess Louise. He was elected Chairman of Overstrand Parish Council in 1904. He exchanged hunting for golf, playing foursomes partnered by the professional at the Royal Cromer Golf Club.

Lady Battersea, too, was solicitous for the poor in the village and was 'Lady Bountiful' to many. On Empire Day all the children at the Belfry School *marched round the large classroom, then each stood in front of Lady Battersea and held out both hands. If they were clean, she placed an apple in one and a penny in the other.*[15] They were also given the Battersea Medal. To some, however, who had no direct contact with her, she was considered a remote figure who was not above sending a cottager a letter if she thought their front garden did not meet her standards of tidiness.

The Rothschilds entered the circle of Edward, Prince of Wales, later King Edward VII, partly through her cousin Nathaniel. He became one of the Prince of Wales's first real friends when they were undergraduates together at Cambridge University and spent much time together drag hunting, largely paid for by Natty.[16]

Queen Alexandra and Constance were close personal friends. However, protocol had to be observed. Lady Battersea's chauffeur, the late Harry Curtis, recalled driving her to Sandringham to visit Queen Alexandra. It was strictly forbidden for royalty to set eyes on the chauffeur, but through some mishap, he was seen by the Queen. Lady Battersea had to write and apologise for this lapse of etiquette.

As has been noted, Lord Battersea was a leading radical Liberal. This led to several well known Liberal Members of Parliament with similar views buying houses in the neighbourhood (see Chapter 11).

As the house grew it demanded a garden commensurate with its size. Lord Battersea was *an ardent gardener, a scientific as well as a practical one.*[17] The garden that Lord and Lady Battersea created at the Pleasaunce was described as *probably amongst the best known in the country.*[18]

*When they first bought the two villas in 1888 between them and the
north sea lay a stretch of open land — in which nothing grew higher
on it than a Dock or a Thistle. Now a sweet-scented garden smiles to
the sky, salt airs stirs leaves in broad plantations, red and white Roses
stud smooth lawns, Lilies flower happily in the half-shade of trees, and
pond-flowers are blooming in sylvan lake and pool.*[19]

So far as is known at present, no documentary evidence has survived
to show who was responsible for the design. Lady Battersea recalls *there
was nothing the Princess [Louise] enjoyed more than giving her invaluable
advice concerning the laying out of the gardens.* This seems to imply the
advice was acted upon. Nearly all the evergreens were transported from
Aston Clinton.

The garden was divided by a public road under which a private tunnel
was built. The walls were lined with white tiles, which deterred some
visitors from entering, thinking it led to a lavatory. The garden was also
divided by the footpath which was a continuation of the lane from North
Repps. From this footpath today traces of the original garden can still be
seen. They are indeed *Echoes of History.*

The garden Lord and Lady Battersea created was immortalised
as *The Garden of Dreams* in a description by the prolific novelist Ellen
Thorneycroft Fowler in *Ten Degrees Backwards.*

*It was a garden of infinite variety and of constant surprises, where
nothing grew but the unexpected; but where the unexpected flourished
in great profusion and luxuriance.*

The main features included a sunken or Italian garden in which
only pink and purple flowers were grown, *a Japanese garden of streams
and pagodas and strange bright flowers.* The fruit garden was described
as *ideal, where the pear trees and the apple trees were woven into walls and
arches and architraves of green and gold.* In one part of the garden there
was a glade 130 yards long planted principally with trees and shrubs of
a golden tint, intermingled with purple leafed plants, especially various
kinds of Japanese and other maples. The culmination of the garden was
the great herbaceous border 80 yards long, between a path nine to ten
feet in width. The edging was comprised of low irregular rockwork in
which were planted a variety of Alpines. It has been described as *a not a
rainbow in the sky, but on the ground.*

The full extent of the property is shown in a recently discovered plan in the Battersea archive at the Pleasaunce dated 7th April, 1907. It is interesting to note that the plan of the sunken garden is markedly different from that shown on the later estate plans, suggesting the present sunken garden is not to the original design. The 1907 plan depicts Cliff Road coming to an end some way short of the cliff top.[20]

The garden was opened to the public on some Sunday afternoons. Dogs and perambulators were not permitted. It was not unknown for Lord Battersea to absent himself to visit his friend the Hon. Augustine Birrell at the Pightle, Sheringham, on such afternoons.

Both Lord and Lady Battersea had a propensity for friendship and many friends. The original semi-detached villas had been enlarged for the purpose of entertaining. Even before the enlargement there were visitors. One of the first was their old friend, John Morley, later Viscount Morley, who wrote in 1914: *The happiest days of my life were passed in the early times of the Pleasaunce, delightful days of friendship, gaiety, reading, and talks of serious things.*[21]

Every local lodging house would be filled, while the The Cottage was lent to friends or others stayed as guests, including members of Cyril's family. From the earliest days Lady Battersea kept a Visitors' Book, which she called *that precious possession, containing autographs of so many honoured and beloved friends, men and women, — some, alas, who have passed away from this earth.*

One of the first names to appear was Princess Louise, the fourth daughter of Queen Victoria. Princess Louise had much in common with Lady Battersea. It is known she visited the Batterseas as early as September, 1890. Mention has already been made of the way in which the marriages of the Rothschild sisters broke the barriers of tradition. The marriage of Princess Louise in 1871 was even more revolutionary. The first three of Victoria's daughters had married German princes. Her eldest her son, Albert Edward, later, King Edward VII, had married into the Danish royal family. Princess Louise found the idea of marrying a German prince distasteful. She wanted to live in England. Queen Victoria's enthusiasm for German princes was also waning. She wrote to the Prince of Wales:

Times have much changed; great foreign alliances are looked upon as causes of trouble and anxiety, and are of no good. What could be more

painful than the position in which our family were placed during the
wars with Denmark, and between Prussia and Austria.[22]

On 21st March, 1871, Princess Louise married the Marquess of Lorne, heir to the Dukedom of Argyll. She was the first royal Princess to marry outside royalty since Mary Tudor, daughter of Henry VII, married Charles Brandon, Duke of Suffolk in 1515.

Princess Louise was an exceptional person:

… exuberant power of enjoyment, her freedom from any conventionally
Royal consciousness had a social potency which rivalled her mother's
but with this antipodal difference that the Queen evoked awe and
almost paralytic reverence whereas her daughter exhaled physical
ozone.[23]

Lord Lorne and his brother, Lord Archibald Campbell, had been undergraduates together at Trinity College, Cambridge, with Cyril Flower whom they nicknamed 'Flos'. It was to this friendship that Constance attributed her friendship with Princess Louise on a more intimate level than might otherwise have been the case and of being associated with the Princess in many good works. At the time of the Princess's first visit, 'The Cottage' lacked privacy. Constance described it as *Cyril Flower's cliff-side cottage, with its pretty verandah and garden of poppies.* The Princess took tea on the small lawn under the eyes of the fishermen's wives hanging out their washing. She brought her paint box, brushes and a sketch book, determined to thoroughly enjoy herself. She took unattended walks along the beach and bought her own stamps in the village post office. She revelled in the freedom Overstrand offered from the constraints of royalty. It is known that the Prince and Princess of Wales dined at the Pleasuance.[24]

The names of many famous men and women adorned the pages of Lady Battersea's visitor's book. One of the names to occur most frequently was that of Lady Dorothy Nevill. Lady Battersea introduces her in her own words:

In turning over the pages of the Visitor's Book I see in rather large
and uneven calligraphy, recurring year after year, a name that was
well known in the social life of London during the greater part of
the last century [19th], that of Lady Dorothy Nevill, a scion of the

Norfolk house of Walpole. Hers was a remarkable personality. She was invariably true to herself.

Lady Dorothy was born at 11, Berkeley Street, London in 1826. The property was lost shortly afterwards to Henry Baring through gambling. She was brought up at the family home of Wolterton Hall, near Aylsham. In 1847 she married her cousin Reginald Henry Nevill Nevill at Wickmere Church and was buried there sixty-five years later.

Lady Dorothy lived through an age when the English aristocracy, who thought they had an inalienable right to govern, saw itself stripped of its privileges and the franchise extended. She long retained traditional convictions. She *spoke the purest, the best English of two generations ago, but preserved the habit of saying 'Dook' for' Duke, 'yaller' for 'yellow' and 'charlot' for 'chariot'.* She also followed the old aristocratic habit of dropping the initial 'h' and the last 'g'. On one occasion she was staying at the Pleasaunce, when Lady Speyer from Sea Marge called in to play the violin. At the conclusion of the performance she was heard to mutter, *I 'ate that scrathcin' sound.*

She deplored the habit of the *weekend visit*, which grew in popularity as the century progressed. As a protest against this innovation she held her celebrated Sunday lunches. As she knew every statesman, poet, and artist of note from Lord Palmerston onward, many famous guests attended these lunches, including Benjamin Disraeli, Lord Randolph Churchill and Field Marshall Lord Wolesley. Her system of issuing invitations has been described as *discriminately indiscriminate.*[25] Her friendship with Lady Battersea, who was an advanced radical Liberal, may at first seem strange. However, they had one thing in common: both were autocrats. Her memory and powers of observation were legendary and her observations acute. In her memoirs she illustrates two of the social attitudes recorded previously in these pages. It will be recalled that Vice Admiral Lukin deplored the threat of growing equality among the classes. It would seem that the Admiral had cause for worry. Lady Nevill recorded the following:

In the year 1832, an elderly couple, peacefully sleeping in their four-poster, were one morning roughly aroused at an early hour by their excited maid-servant, who, bursting into the bedroom bawled out 'It's passed! It's passed!' Extremely annoyed, the old lady called out from

inside the bed curtains, 'What's passed you fool?' 'The Reform Bill,'
shouted the girl, and 'we're all equal now.'

In her diary, Rachel Ketton of Felbrigg Hall commented on a visit of
the Prince of Wales to Gunton. She noted that when the estate workers
were given half a day off to see the Prince arrive at Gunton station,
they stood in silence as he arrived. She and her husband had not been
invited. The source of their wealth was due to trade, looked down on
in aristocratic society. One stickler to this convention was old Lady
Caroline Suffield — known as 'Double Dow' — of Blickling Hall. Lady
Nevill recalled:

> On one occasion, when present at an assembly at Aylsham, she was
> horrified to discover that two local men, sons of a successful miller and
> merchant of that place, had obtained admission, and it was not long
> before she gave a very pointed demonstration of her resentment by
> exclaiming in a loud voice, 'It is most unpleasant here. I can hardly see
> across the room for the flour dust'.[26]

No visitor to the Pleasaunce reflected the quality of friendship more
deeply than the Honourable Emily Lawless. Lady Battersea described
her as *one of our dearly loved visitors, a very gifted woman, whose literary
ability could rise at times to genius.* The Hon. Emily Lawless was *a born
rebel* with red gold hair, full of laughter and energy, who rejected a
conventional life for the love of wildlife and wild landscapes. She *was
an exile from Ireland, from her own past as a passionate lyricist 'of the
wild Atlantic lands'.*[27] Her natural element was the sea. She was a strong
swimmer and fearless diver. Lord Battersea built a room for her he called
the Gate House overlooking the sea where she could write in peace and
meditate. It still stands today. Sadly, her health deteriorated before she
could make use of the facility. Her most celebrated book of poetry is
entitled *With the Wild Geese*, 1902. In 1904 she was awarded an Honorary
Doctorate of Literature in Dublin.

In 1907 she left the following Valediction to Lady Battersea after a
visit to the Pleasaunce:

> *Farewell again, truest, most helpful soul!*
> *This world is dearer to me for thy sake;*
> *No jot or tittle of its varying whole*

Is worth what love and loving friendship make.
A broader summer track in life is thine,
A narrower, shade-infested, mine,
Yet over, both, methinks, the same stars shine.

Another well known woman who stayed at the Pleasaunce was Mrs. Mary Benson, whom W.E. Gladstone described as *the most intelligent woman in Europe* and in the words of Dame Ethel Smythe was the matriarch of *an unpermissibly gifted family.* Her late husband was the first Headmaster of Wellington College, later first Bishop of Truro and Archbishop of Canterbury. Her five children were all brilliant in their spheres of life, but none ever married.

Her youngest, son, E.F. Benson, was a regular visitor to the Pleasaunce in August. At the conclusion of his stay there, he moved a few hundred yards up Pauls Lane to stay with Sir George and Lady Lewis at the Danish Pavilion. His trunk was placed in a wheel barrow and pushed up the road.

Among the many men who stayed at the Pleasaunce were those who had reached the peak of their profession. These included Field Marshall Viscount Garnet Wolseley, one time Commander-in-Chief of the army; George Meredith, the doyen of English literature, who stayed at the Pleasaunce in the summer of 1896 and 1897; George Curzon, with his beautiful American wife, the former Mary Leiter, stayed there prior to taking up his appointment as Viceroy of India in late October, 1899. George Curzon was the only one of her many guests whom Lady Battersea mildly criticised: his *conversation could be both sparkling and amusing, his uncommon personality being a little spoilt by a somewhat dictatorial manner and phraseology.* The celebrated lawyer Lord Halsbury and Lord Rayleigh, the eminent Victorian scientist, whose wife was Arthur Balfour's sister, were other visitors. Joseph Hodges Choate, the popular American Ambassador to the Court of St. James, 1899–1905, who did much to foster America–British relations was another visitor.

Prominent ecclesiastical persons figure on the list of visitors. These included Dr. Maclagan, the Archbishop of York, the Bishop of Norwich, for whom a room was kept, and Canon Jessop. An old friend of Lady Battersea since his undergraduate days at Cambridge University since meeting at a cricket match at Aston Clinton was the Reverend Edward Lyttelton, later Headmaster of Eton College, 1905–1916. He and wife and two small children renewed their friendship with Lady Battersea when he stayed in Cromer. Mrs. Lyttelton bought a plot of land on the boundary of Overstrand and Sidestrand where her house known as Grange-Gorman was built (See Chapter 9).

It is still possible from existing letters and diaries to gain an insight into life at the Pleasaunce during the time that Lord and Lady Battersea lived there together. Constance never lost her early unbridled admiration of Cyril's beauty. When he was present she had eyes and ears for no one else. At the Pleasaunce this expressed itself through her admiring glances, in calling him duckie or lovie, and in laying a hand upon his head as she passed his chair.

> He was coming up across the garden one morning from his early bathe, dressed in the bright colours he affected, a green tam-o'-shanter, a blazer, a pink shirt, and as she approached the loggia where we were breakfasting, she could not curb her fervour. 'Does not dearest Cyril look too beautiful this morning?' she cried. 'Dearest Cyril I was saying how beautiful you looked!'[28]

A letter from Raymond Asquith to a friend dated August, 1898, provides an unusual insight into life at the Pleasaunce. Asquith was invited for what he thought was a traditional weekend house party. It turned out to be something very different: the house is reeking with the gross and human odours which ever cling to the skirts of philanthropy: one sits down to a rabble of small shopkeepers from Balham and Battersea.[29] The occasion was the annual cricket match between Lord Battersea's Overstrand employees and the tenants on Lord Battersea's Battersea estate.

> They actually want me to play cricket with them tomorrow! He suffers terribly from his wife who is full of philanthropy and temperance and all that sort of nonsense, and while she is entertaining the good templars and prison matrons and heavens knows what horrors down in Buckinghamshire, and here they are eating and drinking and talking their curious dialect and exhaling a poisonous atmosphere of retail religion through one of the most beautiful houses in Norfolkshire.[30]

This letter also throws some light upon the gracious character of Lord Battersea:

And my host, hating them like death, but moving among them like a radiant god, the epitome of everything that is beautiful, luxurious and refined, and treating them all with a cordiality that does infinite credit to his forbearance.

Five years later in January, 1903, Sidney and Beatrice Webb spent the best part of a fortnight staying on the Battersea estate in Overstrand. The mornings were spent working on their social interests. In the afternoons they walked on the beach or occasionally rode and in the evenings they read eighteenth-century literature. Sidney and Beatrice were joined for a week by their old friends Graham Wallas[31] and his wife, who stayed with them. Mr. and Mrs. George Bernard Shaw stayed at the big hotel nearby. Beatrice wrote in her diary, *Three delightful evenings we spent listening to GBS reading his new work — the Superman. To me it seems a great work, quite the biggest thing he has done.*

Beatrice Webb wrote a frank appraisal of the characters of Lord and Lady Battersea as she saw them:

Half a dozen times we went for a chat with our neighbours in their resplendent villa, or Lady Battersea came to see us. She is a good and true-hearted woman and quite intelligent, though like all these 'Society Dames' quite incapable of anything but chit-chat, flying from point to point. He is distinctly objectionable, a man without either intellect or character, and I should imagine with many bad habits of body and mind — a middle-class Croesus, ex-Adonis, ennobled for party purposes, a most unpleasant type of functionless wealth. They live in a gorgeous villa filled overflowing with objects of virtue and art, with no individuality or taste.[32]

These strictures seem a little hard on Lord Battersea. They take no account of his disappointment at not being to assume the Governorship of New South Wales, nor his charity work as one of the founders of the Recreation Evening Classes and as treasurer of the Metropolitan Hospital, London.

Violet Asquith, daughter of the future Prime Minister H.H. Asquith, and younger sister of Raymond above, wrote from the Pleasaunce to her friend Hugh Godley a letter dated 28th December, 1905. She was then eighteen years old.

My dear Hugh, ... Beb and Oc [her older brothers Herbert and Arthur]
and I are staying here with Ld Battersea — do you know him? he's an
odd character narrow & violent & personal in politics — intensely
generous in private life; very rich and childless & fond of pictures &
gardening & devoted to all of us whom he has known since we were
born and still treats us as if we were 6 & 7. He has only just left off
kissing Beb! & provides crackers and Xmas trees for us every day.

The house is warm and dark and scented with low wide yielding sofas
& jars full of rose leaves & spikenard & oriental curtains shutting off
room from room. We play gambling games like sympathy & antipathy
& 30 & quarante after & Connie always loses.[33]

The last years of Lord Battersea's life were dogged by ill health. He
suffered from diabetes and died of pneumonia on 27th November,
1907, aged 68. On 4th December Overstrand Parish Council passed the
following resolution:

We the members of the Parish Council of Overstrand beg to offer to
Lady Battersea the expression of their deepest sympathy and most
sincere condolence in her great bereavement and to assure her that her
grief is shared by the people of the Parish and neighbourhood.

The late Lord Battersea as Chairman of the Council for many years
rendered most valuable services to the civic interests of the community.
The people have suffered a loss which it is difficult to overestimate. His
acts of loving kindness are known and acknowledged in many homes.

He was buried in the churchyard of the ruined mediaeval church
of St Martin's, Overstrand, near the south porch.[34] On his tomb were
inscribed words by Walter Savage Landor:

Nature I loved and next to nature Art
I warmed both hands before this fire of life.
It sinks, and I am ready to depart.

After Lord Battersea's death, Lady Battersea continued living at the
Pleasaunce much as before, entertaining in season and deeply involved in
her philanthropic works. The story is still related in Overstrand that Queen
Alexandra visited Lady Battersea at the Pleasaunce, and was refused entry
by an over-zealous servant. Here is an account of that incident in a letter

dated 4th August, 1911, written from Sandringham to Lady Battersea by Charlotte Knollys, Queen Alexandra's trusted Lady-in-Waiting:

Dear Lady Battersea,

When your telegram arrived I was just going to begin this letter to tell you from the Queen how much she enjoyed her visit to the Pleasaunce — her only regret was that you were not there yourself. The Dowager Empress [of Russia] accompanied the Queen and they were both perfectly delighted with the place really looked too beautiful for words, and Sir D. Probyn, who as you know is a great gardener himself was in raptures. At first we were — very properly — refused admittance! The Queen rang the bell and on the door being opened she said 'I should like to see the place,' and the servant — I think it was a footman — answered — 'I am afraid you cannot.' 'Oh yes', says the Queen, 'I am a great friend of your mistress,' but still he was obdurate, taking the party no doubt for 'Trippers', upon which Sir Dighton came forward and whispered in his ear who it was! Then your head man came and the gardener and nothing could exceed the civility of everyone. We had brought our own tea and they provided hot water, and I personally have seen the place twice before, but the beauty of it this time struck me more than I can possibly tell you.[35]

Throughout her life Lady Battersea was motivated by philanthropic ideals. These she inherited from her mother: *Dear mother made us realise that we should learn to take our greatest pleasure in trying to help others to a fuller and happier life.*[36] Her philanthropic work is beyond the scope of this book, but it should be recorded that in 1901 she was appointed President of the National Union of Women Workers. The aim of the Union *was to focus all branches of women's work, religious, educational, scientific, philanthropic, social and industrial, to establish a common bond of interest between workers.*[37] This illustrates the breadth of her interests and her liberal attitudes.

Although never formally converting to Christianity, Lady Battersea was influenced by Christian spirituality and worshipped frequently in Overstrand parish church. Lady Constance Battersea died at 6 a.m. on Sunday, 22nd November, 1931, aged 88 years. Canon Carr, The Rector of Overstrand, prefaced his sermon later that morning with these words:

Constance, Lady Battersea, from her 'Reminiscences'.

It is with true sorrow and a deep sense of loss that we have heard that Lady Battersea has passed away. For over forty years she has been living amongst us. She loved Overstrand, and by her kind thought and sympathy has endeared herself to us all. Her great concern was the good of the people and she ever sought to promote their true interests and welfare. We know what a keen interest she always took in the school and how much she did to encourage the teachers and the children in very many ways. Her going leaves a blank in many lives which it will be difficult to fill.

1   Constance Battersea, *Reminiscences* (London: Macmillan, 1922), p. 167.
2   Battersea, p. 166.
3   Lucy Cohen, *Lady de Rothschild and her Daughters, 1821–1931* (London: John Murray, 1935), p. 169.
4   John Cooper, *The Unexpected Story of Nathaniel Rothschild* (London: Bloomsbury, 2015), p. 36.
5   Battersea, p. 180.
6   Gunton papers in the Norfolk Record Office, GTN 3/1/14/8.
7   Annie Berlyn (Mrs. Alfred Berlyn), *Vera in Poppyland* (London: Jarrold, 1891), p. 18.
8   Pleasaunce: a secluded part of a garden, laid out with trees and walks.
9   Battersea, p. 329.
10 Jane Brown, *Lutyens and the Edwardians: an English architect and his clients* (London: Viking, 1996), p. 94.
11 Christopher Hussey, *The Life of Sir Edwin Lutyens* (London: Country Life, 1950), pp. 68, 72.
12 Joan Bradfield, *Overstrand Chats* (Overstrand: St. Martin's Church), p. 6.
13 E.F. Benson, *Final Edition* (London: Longmans, Green, 1940), p. 46.

14   *The Spectator*, 17th December 1892.

15   Bradfield, p. 3.

16   Jane Ridley, *The Heir Apparent* (London: Chatto & Windus, 2012; Random House, 2013), p. 61.

17   Battersea, p. 329.

18   *The Gardener's Chronicle*, 7th October 1911, p. 260.

19   Frances A. Bardswell, *Sea-Coast Gardens and Gardening* (London: Sherratt and Hughes, 1908).

20   It was not until 1912 that Lady Battersea gave land to form the loop that joins Cliff Road to Pauls Lane. I am grateful to Mr. Geoffrey Kidd for this information.

21   Battersea, p. 173.

22   E.F. Benson, *Queen Victoria's Daughters* (New York: Appleton-Century, 1938), p. 163.

23   Benson, Queen Victoria's Daughters, pp. 167—168.

24   Bradfield, p. 3.

25   Ralph Nevill, *The Life & Letters of Lady Dorothy Nevill* (London: Methuen, 1919), p. 108.

26   Ralph Nevill (ed.), *Leaves from the Notebooks of Lady Dorothy Nevill* (London: Macmillan, 1910), p. 45.

27   Brown, p. 58.

28   Benson, *Final Edition*, p. 50.

29   John Jolliffe, *Raymond Asquith: life and letters* (London: Collins, 1980), p. 42.

30   Jolliffe, p. 42.

31   Well known socialist and Fabian and co-founder of the London School of Economics.

32   Beatrice Webb, *The Diary of Beatrice Webb* ed. Norman and Jeanne MacKenzie, vol. 3 (London: Virago, 1984), p. 267.

33   Violet Bonham Carter, *Lantern Slides: the diaries and letters of Violet Bonham Carter, 1904—1914* ed. Mark Bonham Carter and Mark Pottle (London: Weidenfeld and Nicolson, 1996), pp. 94—95.

34   The church was later restored and is still in use.

35   Cohen, p. 283.

36   *Lady de Rothschild: extracts from her notebooks, with a preface by her daughter Constance Battersea* (London: Arthur L. Humphreys, 1912), p. 17

37   Battersea, p. 440.

9

Celebrities 1: Literati

The publication of Clement Scott's article in the *Daily Telegraph* in the late summer of 1883 led immediately to the arrival in Poppyland of well known members of the artistic community, followed in due course by many celebrities. The first visitors were Theodore Watts Dunton and Algernon Swinburne. Owing to his deteriorating condition, Swinburne had gone to live with Watts Dunton in 1879 at his home of The Pines, 11, Putney Hill, where he stayed until his death. History is indebted to the keen observation of Clara Watts Dunton for insight into their visits to the Norfolk coast.

Swinburne read the *Daily Telegraph* while Watts Dunton patronised *The Times*, which Swinburne could not bear on account of what he called its *We-ishness*, referring to the leading article. On reading Scott's article in August 1883, Swinburne commented *this must be a really delicious sort of place*, adding, *in spite of this worthy man's florid style of Cockney enthusiasm*. Having read the article, Watts Dunton, too, expressed an interest in seeing Poppyland. By the middle of September they had left for Cromer and had put up at the Bath Hotel. Swinburne regarded Cromer as a *rather esplanady sort of place*. (The Bath Hotel was actually situated on the Promenade.) This was Swinburne's way of saying Cromer did not meet his exacting requirements. The only places that appealed to him had to be secluded and quiet, to be within easy reach of the sea with a sandy beach giving rise to deep water bathing at all tides and the lodgings in which they stayed must be free from all visitors apart from those from The Pines. *It was of the utmost importance that Swinburne's bathing place would permit of his plunging into the water 'in puris naturalibus'.*[1] More generally another factor which weighed considerably with Watts Dunton and Swinburne was the awe-inspiring interest of any part of the coastline overlooking a part of the sea covering submerged territory. For this reason Suffolk and Norfolk were preferred to other counties.

By 18th September the two friends were installed in the Mill House at Sidestrand. Swinburne wrote to his sister *yesterday we left the Metropolitan splendours of Cromer for the delicious little refuge from which I write*. When Watts Dunton and Swinburne arrived they found a *surprise packet* waiting for them. It proved to be *a most fervent description* of the countryside. It was unsigned. On being interrogated Louie Jermy volunteered the information that the previous occupant of the room, who had left the day before, was none other than Clement Scott. Swinburne commented:

> *Is it not funny that we should have got into the very house occupied till last evening by the man who unconsciously induced us to come into the country?*

Both Watts Dunton and Swinburne came to love the peace and quiet of the Mill House with its riot of flowers and neat little lawn. It was the genius of Louie Jermy that she was able to make two such different people happy. Alfred Jermy and Swinburne became firm friends. On summer evenings Swinburne read his proofs aloud to his host. The depths of the friendship may be seen in the concluding lines of Swinburne's poem *The Mill Garden* which reflect his love of the Mill House and garden:

> *Friend, the home that smiled us welcome hither when we came,*
> *When we pass again this summer, surely should reclaim*
> *Somewhat given of heart's thanksgiving more than words fulfil -*
> *More than song, were song more sweet than all but love, might frame.*
> *Fair befall the fair close that lies below the mill.*

By the time Clara Watts Dunton met Swinburne he was unable to stay at the Mill House as the cliffs were too steep for him to climb up from the beach. Another lodging was procured *some little distance* west of Cromer on the Runton Road. Swinburne probably used the West Runton gap in order to reach the beach. Clara Watts Dunton recorded that Swinburne gave orders for a boatman to row him some distance from the land in order he could dive into deep water. He enjoyed the dive but got into the boat cold and exhausted. On a second attempt he came out almost blue with cold and was forced to abandon swimming for walking about the beach and looking with longing at the sea.

Swinburne was a member of the Unity Club. Another member of that club who was an early visitor to the Mill House was George R. Sims. Sims was one of the most remarkable men to visit Poppyland:

> He lives every hour of the day in a fever heat of exciting work and thrilling adventure. His energy is simply astounding, and to see the mass of material he turns out in the course of a day is enough to create a panic in the mind of the hardest hustler yet born.[2]

George Robert Sims, 1847–1922, was the eldest of the six children of George Sims, a London merchant, and his wife, Louise Amelia Ann. His mother was the daughter of the Chartist leader, John Dinmore Stevenson, who in retirement lived with the family. She was President of the Women's Provident League which had feminist leanings. She was an ardent theatre goer. Thus early in life he was influenced by progressive thinking which helped to shape the future course of his life.

There are many parallels between the lives of George Sims and Clement Scott. At an early age Sims was taken to the theatre, as was Scott. He cut his journalist teeth on writing for such publications as Fun. Like Scott, he owed much of his success to joining a London club. Sims was in London with a party of friends when one said he knew an awfully jolly place, where they could smoke and drink decent liquor. This turned out to be Unity Club which was a bit of old fashioned Bohemia and the haunt of actors, authors and journalists. It was situated between Wych Street and the Strand. This was to be my jumping-off place for the world of authorship, wrote Sims. In his early years he was able to combine journalism and play writing with working in his father's firm in Aldersgate. He joined forces with Clement Scott in the play Jack in the Box, which was produced at the Strand Theatre on 7th February, 1887. Sims was one of London's most successful playwrights. He was the first author to have four plays running simultaneously in London.

In 1877 a new Sunday periodical was published entitled the Referee which was widely read. From the first Sims wrote a weekly article under the title Mustard and Cress, using the pseudonym Dagonet. His Mustard and Cress articles brought Sims considerable fame. He was consulted by correspondents on every possible subject. In an interview with Clement Scott's second wife, Sims recorded that he resorted to long walks in exasperation as his volume of correspondence increased:

I love outdoor exercise. I often tramp as far as Barking and back, or anywhere down in the slums and by-streets of this great, grimy city of our ours where I can mix with the crowd of 'Sweated London', and study the lives of these half-starved creatures. Oh, those poor pinched faces of the hungry, wailing little ones! They would make your heart ache to see them. These children do not live, my dear friend, they only linger.[3]

He used his articles to bring Poppyland to the attention of a wider public:

Overstrand is a charming combination of green fields, blue seas and rugged cliffs, and has a great future before it. I strongly recommend anyone who wants perfect rest and glorious air amid beautiful scenery to try Overstrand. There is something in the air that makes you want to lie on the grass and let the world go by.[4]

The success of his play *The Lights o' London* in London, the provinces and America, enabled Sims to devote himself to those social questions in which he was deeply interested. He joined a society that devoted itself to the improvement of working-class conditions in the Borough, south London. A school board officer offered to show him the worst areas of poverty. He was appalled by what he saw. Sims wrote a series of articles entitled *How the Poor Live,* illustrated by the artist Fred Barnard. The exposure of how poor *were horded together in the vilest and most insanitary conditions in the capital of the British Empire* touched the public conscience. Sims was asked to give evidence before the Royal Commission on the Housing for the Poor, of which the Prince of Wales was President.

His experiences in south London led Sims to what he called *a life of crime.* It brought him into close touch with some of the perpetrators of the most sensational crimes of the day, including the Jack the Ripper murders. His picture had been printed on the outside cover of his *Social Kaleidoscope.* It was taken to Scotland Yard by a coffee-stall keeper as the likeness of the assassin.

Sims was a friend of the actor Henry Petit, whom he described as *having the gift of the theatre in a remarkable degree.* Petit was as financially successful as any author of his time, leaving nearly £50,000 at the time of his death. He was as much a character as

Sims. These two visited the Mill House and descended upon the quiet lanes of Poppyland. It was not to be expected that two such larger than life characters would not leave their mark in the area - as indeed they did. Sims wrote:

> Our best thanks are due to the good Norfolk folk of Sidestrand and Overstrand, who have let us run wild right through their farmyards and make ourselves at home in their sweet cottage gardens, who have spared no effort to make us happy and comfortable, and who have loaded us with favours. The postmaster at Overstrand has kept the wires open for us at all manner of unreasonable hours, and his kind little wife has flashed our messages to the four corner of the earth with marvellous skill and accuracy. Our return messages from the four corners of the earth have been brought to us in hot haste by rosy-cheeked special messengers as though the fate of empires depended upon them, and even distant Cromer has laid itself out to supply our modest wants with celerity and dispatch, sending such supplies as we requisitioned in the town back to us by mounted messengers or behind the fastest trotting ponies to be had for love or money.

Beckett's post office at Overstrand, from whence wrote G.R.Sims, 'the kind little postmaster's wife has flashed our messages to the four corners of the earth'. Princess Louise purchased her stamps here.

It may have been something to do with the fact that many men found their social lives within the company of other men in clubs, but this was a an era in which practical jokes were commonly practised. While staying at the Mill House Sims feigned lunacy and Pettit pretended to be his keeper. On leaving, Sims wrote:

> We have bidden farewell to Poppyland, and I am not at all sure that Poppyland is sorry. I am afraid our conduct latterly has hardly been in accordance with the peaceful conditions of this sweet Sleepy Hollow. The miller's good wife will probably sleep more peacefully now she knows she will not come down in the morning and find her front door wide open, and hear from neighbours that wild authors have been careering round about the lanes in the small hours plotting murders and yelling at each other, driving the chained watch dogs mad with impotent rage.[5]

The well-known playwright Wilson Barrett was an early visitor to the Mill House. Louie Jermy recalled that while Scott, Sims and Barrett were staying there together, the post brought Barrett a letter which informed him that a play had failed and involved him in a large financial loss. When Louie walked in, he was sitting in a chair on the right-hand side of the fire place, head in his hands, sobbing like a child. Sims broke the tense silence:

> Well, old chap, it's blazing hard luck, he said. There's nothing for it but to call your creditors together and 'go up'!
> No, I'll be damned if I do! I've never let any man in for a farthing in my life, and it's too late to begin that game. I must write another play that shall put things right.

While still staying in the quiet of the Mill House Barrett evolved the outline of the play *The Sign of the Cross*, which proved to be one of the greatest successes in the history of the British stage. Louie *never varied the story*. However, Clement Scott's second wife gave a different version of events. She wrote that Wilson Barrett invited her and Clement to dinner in London. They met at Gatti's restaurant in the Strand where Barrett unfolded the story *The Sign of the Cross*. Scott was most enthusiastic. They discussed the plot together and Barrett suggested that Scott should do the *polishing*.

Poppyland attracted some of the leading actors and actor/managers of the day. While staying in Cromer many of them gave entertainments in aid of the Cromer Hospital.

George Alexander, later Sir George, distinguished actor/manager of the St. James's Theatre where he produced *Lady Windermere's Fan*, spent summer months over several years at the turn of the century in North Lodge Cottage, Cromer, or Overstrand. Lutyens prepared a preliminary design for a house for Alexander in Overstrand, but the scheme was never executed. Dr. Dent visited him professionally one afternoon when Alexander remarked that there were many good actors staying in the neighbourhood at that time.

Dr. Dent, Cromer physician and medical man to famous visitors. His memoirs are an invaluable source of information.

Dent told him he was the fourth distinguished actor he had seen that day. Alexander replied he knew Dent was looking after Henry Irving and John Hare, but who was the fourth? Dr. Dent watched his face closely when he replied, *Arthur Roberts!* Roberts was a fine artist, but not a great actor in the highest sense of the term. Roberts was now touring the east coast. He had a car accident while travelling from Yarmouth to Cromer for his next engagement.

Herbert Beerbohm Tree was manager of the Haymarket Theatre and later of His Majesty's Theatre. In 1887 Mr. and Mrs. Herbert Beerbohm Tree, with their daughter Viola and her nanny, were staying in the same suite at Tucker's Hotel, Cromer, just vacated by the Empress of Austria, waiting for George R. Sims and his party to vacate the Mill House.

Mrs. Beerbolm Tree recorded:

'Poppyland.' I remember it was the Alexanders who told us of its advantages; therefore hither we repaired — with much preamble and

perambulators (I expect I went first, for such arrangements were left to me until they broke down; then, all our life together, Herbert, once appealed to, could instantly repair disasters). Cromer, in those days, a huge church, two tiny streets and sea! At first the hotel — half cliff, half inn, with many stages and no particular recommendations - then a lodging search, which bequeathed us the landlady joke, 'You'll get a loverly view of the rail-way station.' The town having failed us, we repaired to the ruined church, poppied cliff and one cottage which constituted Overstrand. We took the cottage, dreamed in the ruined church, drowsed on the cliff. Viola was an amazing child with waves and sand: Herbert as amazing as Poseidon. The sea seemed to belong to him and her.

Squire Bancroft, who visited Cromer, was one-time manager of the Prince of Wales and Haymarket Theatres.

Henry Irving, who was manager of the Lyceum theatre, was considered the greatest actor of his time. Some indication of his fame can be gauged from a description of his second tour of America in the spring of 1885. *So ends the most astonishing professional progress any actor has ever made in this country*[6], wrote one of the foremost of American journalists.

None of those who stood with Mr. Irving and Miss Terry on the deck of the 'Arizona', while the figures of the friends who waved a last farewell from the quay gradually faded from sight, will ever lose from their hearts the echo of the cheers which seemed like a breath of 'immortal air' wafting them on their homeward way.[7]

Clement Scott considered playing Becket was Irving's greatest role: *I am inclined to think that Becket is the very greatest of Sir Henry Irving's*

Sir Henry Irving, the first British actor to be knighted, in his role as Becket, as featured in Mrs Clement Scott's 'Old Days in Bohemian London'.

stupendous achievements at the Lyceum, he wrote. Sir Henry Irving was a regular visitor to Poppyland, staying at the Links Hotel, sometimes with his friend, John Hare. Mrs. Edith Alec-Tweedie recalls sitting next to him at dinner one evening in London. He was suffering from a cold and bronchitis, but made light of it: *'Oh, it is really nothing, and I am off tomorrow to Cromer where it will all blow away!*[8] Three months later he was dead. He was playing Becket at the time. It is believed the last photograph ever taken of Sir Henry Irving was taken at The Grange, Pauls Lane, Overstrand.

Sir John Hare was actor/manager of the Garrick Theatre. He built his own house in Overstrand, which he called The Grange. It was built almost opposite the newly erected Danish Pavilion, the summer residence of his friends, Sir George and Lady Lewis (See chapter 12). It was referred to at the time as *Hare's beautiful house near Cromer.* Sir John Hare was one of the most distinguished actors of his generation. He excelled in old men's parts and was recognized as the greatest character actor of his day. John Hare was often commanded to Windsor or Sandringham. He was very proud of the many gifts he received from royalty, especially a silver cigar box with the representation of a hare chased on it. He commented *I value this present from King Edward because of the very kind thought of the donor who had gone out of his way to make the gift so entirely personal in character.*[9]

Physically Sir John Hare was not a strong man, suffering from depression. In May, 1903, after returning to London from Overstrand he wrote to Dr. Dent, thanking him for his *kindly skill and care.* Dr. Dent paid this tribute to him:

> Foremost in advocating the claims of the needy of his own calling, John
> Hare was ever a man of most kindly disposition and a generous friend:
> an outstanding figure indeed among the great in his profession.

Sir John Hare found Overstrand too quiet for his tastes. Opposite The Grange is situated an older house. A postcard has recently come to light written from this dwelling dated July 1910, which tells the recipient that John Player, the cigarette manufacturer, has just bought the house opposite.

The actor Edward Compton, 1854–1918, spent the summer of 1890 in Cromer. He was married to the actress Virginia Bateman, a member of the well known acting family. In 1881 he formed the Compton Comedy Company which toured the country playing Shakespeare and English comedies. Among his children were the novelist Compton McKenzie and the actress Fay Compton. Well known for his versatility, agility and entertaining powers as a mimic, Fred. Leslie (born Hobson), visited Cromer. His performances, which included singing, dancing, clowning

Miss Edna May comes into the garden at of her cottage (Carrwood House) at Overstrand, September 1906. 'Since this, Miss May has returned to the hub of the universe, and is agreeably flourishing in the title role of 'The Belle of Mayfair'. The Bystander.

and whistling, were noted for their high spirits and ludicrous charm. Clement Scott called 'one of the great lyric and comic artists of my time.'

A glittering array of actresses visited Poppyland, noteworthy for their beauty and glamour. Ellen Terry was one of the first modern stars of the British stage. In 1878 she joined Henry Irving's company as his leading lady, and for more than the next two decades she was considered the leading Shakespearean and comic actress in Britain. It was a golden period in her career. Two of her most famous roles were Portia in the *Merchant of Venice* and Beatrice in *Much Ado About Nothing*. Her portrait was painted by the leading artists of her day including G.F. Watts and John Singer Sargent. She was a prolific letter writer, famously corresponding with George Bernard Shaw over a long period. Shaw wrote that she had *all the nameless charm, all the skill, all the force, in a word, all the genius.* Ellen Terry frequented Cromer and was friendly with Louie Jermy at the Mill House.

Among other well known actresses to spend time in Poppyland were Edna May, Lillie Langtry and Olga Nethersole. Edna May was a super-star. Born of a humble background in New York, she won fame and fortune by becoming the *Belle of New York.* It is said she *went on to conquer the hearts of not just the Americans and British, but just about the whole world.* Her picture was virtually in every shop in London and every person of consequence wanted to meet her.

Lillie Langtry, like Edna May, conquered the world, but some years before the birth of Poppyland.

> Born into an age of great symbolic personalities, as Tennyson meant poetry, Mr. Gladstone politics, Sarah Bernhardt and Henry Irving the stage, Mrs. Langtry, the 'lily' that suddenly flowered in Jersey, meant Beauty personified; and almost instantly she meant that, not only for London drawing-rooms, but for the whole world.[10]

As a sixteen year old girl she rode in Jersey with the Suffield family. She recorded:

> Among those hibernating visitors were Lord and Lady Suffield and their children, with whom I rode often about the country lanes and knew fairly well. Perhaps the first compliment paid to a girl in her teens lingers longer in the memory than the subsequent petty speeches that may be showered on her. Anyhow, it was Lord Suffield at one of those informal picnics in which Jerseyites delight who made the following remark: 'Do you know, Miss Le Breton, that you are very, very beautiful? You ought to have a season in London'.[11]

There is little doubt this fired her ambition. Her entry into the London season has been described as *an assault on London society,*[12] despite her self-deprecation. She captured the heart of the Prince of Wales. She was acknowledged as his official mistress. He drove with her in an open horse drawn carriage and promenaded with her in public at high profile sporting and social events. It was made discreetly clear to those inviting the Prince to any social occasion that it would be sensible to invite Mrs Langtry also, otherwise he would be extremely unlikely to attend. At Gunton it is well authenticated that the Lord Suffield lent her a shooting box,Elderton Lodge, where she could meet the Prince.[13]

Lillie Langtry made several visits to Poppyland. She formed part of a large house party at Hanworth Hall when let to Lord de Wilton. She also stayed at the Pleasaunce with Lady Battersea. Her daughter, Lady Ian Malcolm, stayed at Knapton Hall, just prior to the outbreak of the Great War.

Olga Nethersole, noted for her beauty, stayed at St. Bennett's in Vicarage Road, Cromer. From 1888 she played important parts in London, at first under Rutland Barrington and John Hare at the Garrick Theatre. She toured Australia and America playing leading parts in modern plays. She served as a nurse in London throughout the first World War and later established the People's League for Health for which she received a Royal Red Cross (RRC) in 1920. She combined the theatre with health work for the rest of her life. She was created a Commander of the British Empire in 1936.

Four well known actresses, all of whom were noted for their beauty, who visited Poppyland, received proposals of marriage from members of the aristocracy, with varying results. These were Emily May Finney, Belle Bilton, Rosie Boote and Rachel Berridge. The subsequent marriages and divorce cases following these proposals created immense public interest at the time.

Emily May Finney was born in Peckham, London, to a coal merchant father. She was educated as a lady, but following her father's business failure she became an actress to support her mother and sister, adopting the name Miss Fortescue. Fortescue first joined the D'Oyly Carte Company at the Opera Comique in London at the age of 19 in April, 1881, in the original production of *Patience*. When the company transferred in the October to the new Savoy Theatre Fortescue moved with it, creating the small role of Celia in *Iolanthe*. She quickly became a favourite with male members of the Savoy's audience. She captured the interest of young Lord Glenmoyle, later the 2nd Earl Cairns, who had seen her on stage in *Iolanthe*. She accepted his proposal of marriage, leaving the Savoy at the end of August 1883. Glenmoyle soon broke off the engagement under pressure from his family. Fortescue sued for breach of promise and was awarded £10,000. With her award she started her own touring theatre company. Dr. Dent met Miss Fortescue and her mother while dining with Mrs. Heilbut, wife of the rubber magnate, at Danecourt, Overstrand.

Belle Bilton and her sister Flo, known as the Sisters Bilton, were well known variety artists. In 1889 Belle secretly married Viscount Dunlo, heir to the Earl of Clancarty, who strongly disapproved of the marriage. Viscount Dunlo was forced to travel abroad, leaving Belle pregnant and penniless, having ended her career on marriage. Encouraged by his father, Viscount Dunlo filed for divorce in a case that created great public interest. After losing the case he returned to live with Belle. Cut off from his allowance, the couple lived on her earnings. At the conclusion of the case Lady Dunlo was asked by an interviewer what verdict she expected. She replied, almost indignantly, *The verdict that was given, simply because I knew I was innocent of the horrible charge that had been trumped up against me.* When asked what she thought of the presiding judge, Sir James Hannan, she replied, *well, all I can say now of his lordship is that he is a dear old chap.* When Belle and her sister appeared on the stage after the trial, the audience stood up and greeted them with prolonged cheering and applause. In 1901 Earl Clancarty died, when the Viscount inherited the title and Belle became the Countess of Clancarty.

Dr. Dent recalls that in later life he met the Countess of Clancarty at Cromer and Flo became Mrs. Evan MacFarlane whom he met frequently at *Tigh-na-mara*, the house built by her mother-in-law in Cliff Avenue, Cromer. Later the property became known as *The Grange* and became the property of Colonel Barclay of Hanworth. It was leased to Mr. John and Lady Agnes Durham, the latter one of the Townshends of Raynham Hall.

On 11th April, 1901, an *immense sensation* was created when the fourth Marquess of Headfort married the Gaiety Girl, Rosie Boote. Rose was a Roman Catholic from a humble background, though she was intelligent and educated in an Ursuline Convent school. The Marquess was a Protestant aristocrat and a Freemason. Great pressure was placed upon them by both families to break off the engagement. The Marquess held a commission as a lieutenant in the First Life Guards. King Edward VII was greatly interested in the affair and told Prince Edward of Saxe-Weimar, the Colonel of the First Life Guards, to do what was possible to prevent the marriage. Prince Edward wrote to Lord Headfort, pointing out that his career would be ruined if he married Miss Boote, as he could not be received by the regiment. The Marquis replied, regretting that he could not see the matter in that way. He sent his resignation papers to Lord Roberts. However, instead of accepting Lord Headfort's resignation, the general ordered the Marquis to hold himself in readiness to go to South Africa on active service. Confronted with the choice of giving up his fiancée or his commission , the Marquis hesitated not and resigned his commission.

In 1904 there was an even bigger sensation, when the Duchess of Westminster invited the couple to the Royal Ball. The entrance of Lord and Lady Headfort was the sensation of the evening. Lady Headfort bore herself in a manner which every one declared to be perfect. Her gown was one of the most beautiful seen at the ball; her appearance was as striking and, if anything, her manners were better than those of the grande dames who crowded around her inquisitively.

After she was married, the Marchioness of Headfort continued to visit Cromer, staying either in Avenue or the Royal Links Hotel. She was described as a *devoted wife and mother, possessing a wonderful business capacity*. In July, 1909, *The Tatler* commented that the *cleverness and charm* of the Marchioness *have gained her great popularity in Irish and London society*. Dr. Dent commented that he felt sure Lord Headfort never for one moment *regrets the determination he showed to act on his judgement in the matter of his marriage*.

On the evening of 7th August, 1901, Dr. Dent received a request from the actress Rachel Berridge, who was staying at the Metropole Hotel, for a prescription for a migraine headache as she was going to London the following day for an important engagement. The following evening she arrived back in Comer on the last train and asked for a repeat prescription. She then apologised and asked for it to be written out a third time, explaining she was no longer Rachel Berridge, but Rachel Clonmore. The important engagement was her marriage to the Earl of Clonmore. He had then left for Ireland to tell his family, while she returned to Cromer. The Earl was a popular member of the Marlborough House Set, known to his intimates as 'Earlie'. *He really rippled with fun.*[14] They became the parents of two beautiful daughters.

It is appropriate to mention at this point the establishment of the Mundesley Sanatorium for the treatment of tuberculosis in 1899 by Dr. F. Burton-Fanning, consultant to the Norfolk and Norwich Hospital. It was built in a quiet, remote spot, away from dust as far as possible. The building was a prefabricated timber frame on a brick base, constructed by Messrs Bolton and Paul of Norwich. Internally it was designed to limit the accumulation of dust. It was the first large centre in England built specifically for open-air treatment of the disease. However, due to its status as a private hospital, Mundesley could only offer treatment to wealthy patients. By 1905 it covered thirty acres. Many of the patients who were treated there had connections with the London theatres. It is believed that the golfer Henry Vardon, who designed the Mundesley golf course, was treated there.

Several well known authors visited Poppyland, among whom were Oscar Wilde and E.F. Benson. Oscar Wilde and his wife, Constance, stayed at Grove Farm in the village of Felbrigg in the summer of 1892. It was a critical time in the life of their marriage. The couple were drifting apart, pulled in different directions by conflicting influences. Oscar was beginning his pursuit of the individual. He had already met and formed a relationship with Lord Alfred Douglas (Bosie), of which at this time Constance knew nothing. Constance was deeply into Christian Socialism with her close friend Lady Georgina Mount-Temple of Babbacombe Cliff, Torquay. Oscar and Constance arrived at Felbrigg on 20th August. *It was to be a time of quiet recuperation, and a time to regain that sense of family which had become diluted by recent activities.* They quickly settled into a routine. The mornings and evenings were devoted to work. Oscar was writing his play *A Woman of No Importance*, while Constance was writing letters and keeping in touch with various societies and causes in which she was interested. They spent the afternoon together and would often walk into Cromer, where they generally came across some friends with whom to have tea. Oscar's work was going well. They decided to extend their stay until September 17th. *It is doing us both so much good, and I am already quite well, I recover as quickly as I get ill,* wrote Constance. Oscar took up golf. Constance wrote to Lady Mount-Temple, *I am afraid Oscar is going to become smitten with the golf mania. He played his first game on the links here yesterday and has joined for a fortnight.*

However, at the end of August events took a different turn. A telegram arrived from Lord Alfred Douglas saying he was coming for a night. Constance had to take her son, Cyril, back to Hunstanton where he was staying. When she returned she found that far from staying for a day,

Lord Alfred had installed himself. He and Oscar went playing golf.

Constance commented to Lady Mount-Temple: *I am becoming what I am told the wives of golfers are called a 'golf widow'.* Constance then headed to Babbacombe Cliff to see Lady Mount-Temple while Oscar stayed at the farmhouse another week to finish *A Woman of No Importance.* Bosie stayed. Unbeknown to Constance he placed *himself at the centre of all aspects of Oscar's life.* Thus ended the last holiday Constance and Oscar Wilde enjoyed together. It was the beginning of the end for Oscar. Less than three years later he lost his libel action against the Marquess of Queensberry, leading to his eventual imprisonment.

The renowned Lillie Langtry.

Poppyland found its way into English literature through the writing of the popular novelist E.F. Benson. Known as 'Fred' by all his family, he was born at Wellington College. Since the time when his father had become Archbishop of Canterbury, who took precedence after the monarch in all state occasions, 'Fred' had been a keen observer of social protocol. As Clement Scott and George Sims before him both attributed their success to membership of a club, so Benson's membership of the University Pitt Club was an important influence in shaping his *habit of confident convivial chatter.*[15] Poised, well connected, single and amusing, he was just the kind of young society man-about-town hostesses invited to their parties, including Mrs. George Lewis at Portland Place, later of Overstrand, and Lady Battersea at the Pleasaunce.

It was inevitable that by its very nature Poppyland would be a location which would appeal to E.F. Benson and feature in his writing. In 1896 Benson published a partly autobiographical novel, *Limitations.* Towards the end of the book one of the principal characters is taken ill and visits Poppyland to stay with a friend to recuperate:

> *Lady Ramsden's house stood on the edge of the short-turfed Norfolk Downs, within a hundred yards of the sea. A mile to the north the*

red-roofed little town of Cromer went trooping down to the shore, with its tall grave tower seeming to confer an air of safety to the whole.

Round the house were rambling, uneven lawns, only half broken in, as it were, and retaining something of the freedom of the grass-clad sandhills, and a satisfying medley of flower beds, full of great hardy plants.[16]

Situated a mile south of Cromer and on the cliff top with a large garden, this description is clearly based upon the Pleasaunce, where Benson stayed. E.F. Benson is remembered today principally for his Mapp and Lucia novels. His novel, *Mrs Ames*, which was published in 1912, was a precursor to these novels. It was important in the author's development *for there emerge more of the qualities which would eventually constitute the Benson cocktail, namely a rich capacity for inventing farcical situations, and a compassion to replace the cynicism of the earlier books.*[17]

The eponymous heroine spends a holiday at Overstrand. It is in the character of Mrs Ames that *one may best discern the evolution of the style which would gleefully erupt eight years later in Queen Lucia.*[18] From the description in the book, Overstrand seems hardly to have changed. The village store, though not the same store, still *sells everything from wooden spades to stamps and sticking plaster. There are still miles of firm sands, when the tide is low and often people prefer to walk along the margin of the sea,* frequently with their beloved dog in attendance.

E.F. Benson, in a picture from Harper's Bazaar.

When Arthur Conan Doyle returned to England from South Africa, having contracted enteric fever, he and the journalist Bertram Fletcher Watson took a golfing holiday, staying at the Royal Links Hotel, Cromer. While there, they dined with Benjamin Bond Cabbell at Cromer Hall,

Cromer Hall in a picture album printed at the end of the 19th century. It certainly seems a fit for Baskerville Hall.

who recounted the tale of the *devil dog that cursed his ancestor, Richard Cabell of Buckfastleigh*, died 1677. Squire Richard Cabell reputedly accused his wife of adultery and a struggle ensued. She fled to nearby Dartmoor but he recaptured and murdered her with his hunting knife. The victim's pet hound exacted revenge by ripping out Cabell's throat. The fictional villain Hugo Baskerville bears a close resemblance to the real life Richard Cabell.

> *The description of Baskerville Hall fits Cromer Hall. Until the storm of 1987 the house also had a yew alley, which is of course a major part of the plot. The coachman who took Conan Doyle to his visit to the house went by the name of Baskerville.*[19]

Sir Arthur Conan Doyle was not the only writer with the capacity to relate a gripping and enduring story who visited Poppyland. *The Prisoner of Zenda*, 1894, has stood the test of time. Its creator was Anthony Hope Hawkins, better known as Anthony Hope, who, with his wife and children, frequently stayed in Overstrand. Sir George Alexander played the part of *Rudolf* in the successful play staged at the St. James's Theatre in 1896.

Two celebrated figures from the world of academia from deeply contrasting backgrounds, who made their home or who stayed in Poppyland, complete this chapter. The first of these was Professor Gilbert Murray and his wife Lady Mary Murray. Gilbert Murray was born an Australian whose family emigrated to England, where he was educated. Between 1889 and 1899 Murray was Professor of Greek at Glasgow University. After 1908 he was Regius Professor of Greek at Oxford University. His wife was Lady Mary Howard, daughter of the Earl of Carlisle, whom he met while visiting Castle Howard. The Murrays leased the house known as Beckhythe, Carr Lane, Overstrand, situated opposite that of Sir Henry Fowler. Lady Battersea wrote:

> On the opposite side of the lane is a small but picturesque house, which was tenanted for a few years by a writer of distinction, no other than Professor Gilbert Murray, with his wife, Lady Mary Howard, who were most interesting neighbours and whose departure I regretted.[20]

The American actress Edna May also leased Beckhythe for one season. Dr. Dent commented:

> What a contrast one noticed between the May and the Murray ménage! — the former associated with frivolity, lavish expenditure and the joie de vivre of the passing moment; the latter with simple living and high thought, and the earnest desire to solve in the best possible manner the various social problems of the day.[21]

Older readers may recall Professor Gilbert Murray as a member of the Brain's Trust team on B.B.C. radio shortly after the end of World War II.

One of Lady Battersea's oldest friends was the Honourable and Reverend Edward Lyttelton, whom she had known since he was an undergraduate at Cambridge University. While staying in Cromer with his young family he visited Lady Battersea at the Pleasaunce. She invited him to give Penny Readings in the village, which proved immensely popular.

Edward Lyttelton was both a distinguished sportsman and scholar. He played cricket for Cambridge University and Middlesex, and represented England at football. He was also a well known scholar, being appointed Headmaster of Eton College in 1905. The Lytteltons acquired a plot of land on the boundary of Sidestrand and Overstrand where they built the house known today as Grange-Gorman.[22] Mrs. Lyttelton supervised the building and furnishing of the house. On his retirement from Eton in 1916, Lyttleton officiated in the parish of Sidestrand in place of the Reverend Ivo Hood, who became an army chaplain. He was married to Christobel, youngest daughter of Sir Samuel and Lady Hoare of Sidestrand Hall. Sadly, she was left a widow.

1   Clara Watts-Dunton, *The Home Life of Swinburne* (London: A.M. Philpot, 1922), p. 182.
2   Margaret Scott (Mrs. Clement Scott), *Old Days in Bohemia London: recollections of Clement Scott* (New York: Frederick A. Stokes Company, 1919), p. 248.
3   Scott, p. 249.
4   Gwen M. Parry, *The Maid of the Mill: Louie Jermy of Poppy-land and her Times, 1864−1934* (Westminster: Gwen M. Parry, 1936), pp. 6−7.
5   Parry, p. 6.
6   *The Theatre* ed. Clement Scott, May 1855, p. 235.
7   *The Theatre*, May 1855, p. 241.
8   Ethel Alec-Tweedie, *My Table-cloths: a few reminiscences* (New York: George H. Doran Company, 1916), p. 102.
     H.C. Dent, *The Reminiscences of a Cromer Doctor: A record of many famous personages, amusing anecdotes and stories of diplomats, actors and others* (Holt: Norfolk Press Syndicate, 192-?), p. 13.
10   Richard le Gallienne, in the introduction to Lillie Langtry, *The Days I Knew* (London: Hutchinson, 1925), pp. v−vi.
11   Lillie Langtry, *The Days I Knew* (London: Hutchinson, 1925), p. 35.
12   Jane Ridley, *The Heir Apparent* (London: Chatto & Windus, 2012; Random House, 2013), p. 248.
13   Ridley, p. 258.
14   Langtry, p. 71.
15   Brian Masters, *The Life of E.F. Benson* (London: Chatto and Windus, 1991; Pimlico, 1993), p. 83.
16   E.F. Benson, *Limitations* (London: Ward, Lock, 1896), p. 272.
17   Masters, p. 190.
18   Masters, p. 235.
19   Benjamin Cabbell-Manners, *Cromer Hall: seat of the Cabbell family*, p. 25.
20   Constance Battersea, *Reminiscences* (London: Macmillan, 1922), p. 368.
21   Dent, p. 10.
22   This is an Irish name. Mrs. Lyttelton was the daughter of the Dean of St. Patrick's Cathedral, Dublin.

10

Celebrities 2: Royalty, Aristocracy, Industrialists

In 1887 the young Compton McKenzie[1] was sitting on the beach at Cromer as a four year old boy when he was conscious of a beautiful woman walking past him holding a parasol. She was Elizabeth, Empress of Austria. She had married the Emperor at the age of sixteen, but she was unable to withstand the pressure and interference of her mother-in-law, using travel, hunting and horse riding as a means of escape. She was making her last visit to England. A whole suite of the annex of Tucker's Hotel situated on the Promenade below the hotel itself was allotted to her.

Lady Battersea recalled being presented to Her Majesty at an evening reception in Vienna in 1873. *The Empress was all in white, with great gleaming knots of emeralds in her wonderful hair.* She was seated next to Lady Dudley. Lord Dudley commented: *there are the two most beautiful women in the world.*

The Empress lived in fear of assassination by poisoning. Every morning her staff fetched newly baked bread from a bakery in Jetty Street where her doctor and members of her staff supervised the baking. The loaves were then wrapped, placed in a basket and a procession carried the bread to Tuckers Hotel in Tucker Street, down the passage and so to the annex. The Empress was equally fastidious about fresh milk. Every morning a cow was led to the cliff edge and milked in front of the Empress's window and the milk passed fresh and warm to her majesty.

She was now fifty years old. Her hunting days were over. The Empress divided her time in Cromer by spending the morning sitting in a rocking rowing boat off-shore, much to the discomfort of her ladies-in-waiting, and going for long afternoon walks, accompanied by her bodyguard,

Elizabeth, Empress of Austria, travelled widely in Europe after the death of her son in a murder-suicide pact with his mistress. In this picture she is dressed for coronation as the Queen of Hungary.

Sergeant Lovick of the Cromer police force. She walked bare-headed, with her hat behind her head tied with a bow round her neck. She carried a fan to protect her both from the sun and from inquisitive eyes.

In one of his articles in *The Referee* George R. Sims recalled meeting the Empress in Cromer.

I don't often go into Cromer, but when I do I imitate the Cromerites, and take to my heels directly I see the imperial party. To tell the truth, we both came round a corner from opposite directions, and ran into each other's arms. Of course, when I say that, I merely use the ordinary form of speech. I blushed a rich cardinal colour, and stammered out my apologies in the best German that my confusion would allow; but the Empress instead of replying, simply stood still and stared at me. The street was narrow — so narrow that the people have to pass sideways — and the situation was most embarrassing. At last I could bear it no longer. There was only one course open to me. I took to my heels and fled up the street. But I hadn't gone many yards when I felt my blazer seized from behind. 'Really your Majesty', I exclaimed, 'I don't understand …' Then I looked round and saw it was not the Empress, but a gentleman of the suite. 'Come to Tucker's' he said, 'her Majesty wants to have a few words with you.'

Sims obediently followed, and was ushered into the apartments of the Empress of Austria. She entered the room with a smile and invited him to sit.

'I owe you an apology,' said her Majesty, 'for staring at you so rudely, especially after the paragraph you wrote in last week's Ref. asking that you might not be mobbed or made a fuss with, but the truth is I did not stare at you because you are DAGONET, but because you are the man I have been trying to find for years.'

The Empress handed Sims a large photograph of a group of people picnicking round a tree in one of the branches of which was a man looking down. That man was no less than Sims himself. The Empress said the photograph caused her a great deal of annoyance. *I made up my mind you were a spy who had concealed himself to overhear our conversation. When I came upon you today I recognised you at once as the man in the photograph.*

Sims then explained what happened:

I had climbed the tree to take a little bird that had fallen out of a nest back to its mother. While I was still up the tree your servants came and spread a picnic underneath, and you all sat down. I stopped where I was, as I am a bad climber, and I was afraid I should cut a ridiculous figure if I came down the tree before an audience, when you were all photographed. When you had all gone I came down and went home. I hadn't the slightest idea that you — for I recognise you as the lady in the group — were an empress, and I beg now to offer you my sincere apologies for spoiling the photograph.

The Empress then asked Sims whether he had lunched, and on being answered in the negative asked him to lunch.

We spent the rest of the day at sea, and among my most pleasant memories will ever be the happy afternoon I passed off Cromer Cliffs with her Imperial Majesty the Empress of Austria. That evening I met the gentleman of the suite in the post-office. He was sending a telegram from the Empress to her husband. The gentleman showed me the message. It was this: - Have just found the man up the Tree. He wasn't a spy. He was a newspaper man. I dare say you have heard of him. His name is DAGONET.

In 1902 and in 1905 the Empress's daughter-in-law, Princess Stephanie, daughter of the King of the Belgians, with her second husband, Count Lonyay, visited Cromer. She became Crown Princess of Austria through her marriage to the heir-apparent of the Habsburg dynasty, Archduke Rudolf. She was famously widowed in 1889 when Rudolf and his mistress were found dead in an apparent murder-suicide pact.

Princess Stephanie was attracted to Cromer because of the visit of her mother-in-law, on both occasions staying at Tudor House in Cliff Avenue. The house was built in 1900. She was attended by Dr. Dent. He recalled the Princess spoke in the kindliest terms of her first father-in-law, the Emperor of Austria, in contrast to the low estimation in which she held her father, the Belgian king, who refused permission for his daughter to visit her dying mother in Brussels. Dr. Dent recalled the Princess and her husband were *exceedingly kind* to him *without the least affectation* and always set him completely at ease when he visited them. After the strictly professional aspect of the visit was over, the Princess lit a cigarette, offered one to Dr. Dent, and reclining in a deck chair in the garden while the Count played the piano, asked the doctor to correct her bad English.

Twenty-six members of her staff crammed into Tudor House. It was so full that the Count was robbed of his best Havana cigars and other valuables. As a result of that theft they went to stay with Lord and Lady Battersea at the Pleasaunce. While staying in Overstrand, both the Princess and her husband were unable to go out owing to a minor illness, which was treated by Dr. Dent. While he was attending them, he was offered the use of their motor car. Dr. Dent recorded:

I accepted the kind offer, and rolled round to see my patients in great style, in the Royal equipage. The chauffeur and footman were both clad in purple and gold, and the colour of the car was bright crimson: it was so large, it could scarcely be contained in some of the narrow lanes I had to travel, so it may be imagined what a magnificent progress was made.

In August and September, 1903, a Far Eastern potentate known as Tungku Bezar from the Malay States stayed at the Royal Links Hotel. His dark skinned entourage occupied one whole floor of the hotel, which was filled with an odour of a distinctly far eastern origin. The Tungku was splendidly attired in bright silk apparel, his head adorned with a black fez decorated with a diamond aigrette. Dr. Dent was impressed and, through an interpreter, requested a photograph.

The Tungku's principal wife was a princess in her own right, a daughter of the Sultan of Jahore. Dr. Dent described her as *young and beautiful with finely chiselled features and wonderful eyes which required no kohl to render them more attractive.* The Princess seldom left the hotel, but on one occasion the Tungku was prevailed upon to take the Princess to the Town Hall where Kreisler was giving a recital. The royal party, the women of whom were heavily veiled, occupied the two front rows. The following day Dr. Dent asked the Princess how she enjoyed the performance. She was not at all favourably impressed, much preferring the more strident music of her own country.

A Cromer–Mundesley local train approaching Overstrand station, circa 1906. Perhaps it was bringing celebrities and visitors from further afield via Cromer. The Royal Links Hotel is on the horizon on the left and Overstrand Hall in the centre.

At 10.30 p.m. on the final night of the visit two horse carriages drove up to Dr. Dent's residence. Six black gentlemen presented Dr. Dent with two large photographs of the Tungku. They were, however, horrified when Dr. Dent hinted to the interpreter that he would readily exchange one photograph of the Tungku for one of the Princess.

Mention has already been made of the visits of Princess Louise to Lady Battersea at the Pleasaunce. In May, 1898, the *Derby Mercury* reported that

> *Princess Victoria of Wales has taken a great fancy to Cromer, which is not to be wondered at, as the surroundings are so beautiful. Cromer had already gained the affection of her Royal Highness's art-loving aunt, Princess Louise, Marchioness of Lorne, and now it is rumoured that the Princess of Wales has fallen in love with it, and wants the Prince to take a large villa there or at Overstrand.*

This evidently did not happen.

The Duke and Duchess of Connaught made several visits to Cromer, staying at the Links Hotel. The Duke was the third son and seventh child of Prince Albert and Queen Victoria. He was appointed tenth Governor of Canada in 1911, by King George V. He was the first royal duke to hold that appointment. The Duke and Duchess were known to Dr. Dent from his days as an army doctor in India.

Other members of the aristocracy to visit Cromer, particularly during the early years of the last century, included representatives of the Marquisates of Bath, Salisbury, Lincolnshire, Abergavenny and Worcester; the Earldoms of Pembroke, Carnarvon, Denbigh, Chichester and Rosslyn; the Viscountcies of Hampden, Powerscout, and Goshen; the Baronies of Kintore, Iveagh, Hastings, Tollemache, Grimthorpe, Wimborne, Monkswell and Blythswood.

A number of well known figures from the world of engineering or business stayed in Poppyland or bought second homes in the area. In 1898 work began on the construction of the world's largest civil engineering work to date in the shape of the first Aswan Dam in lower Egypt. The River Nile was Egypt's main artery. At the turn of the century, agricultural production was failing to keep up with the needs of the population. The banks of the Nile needed to be controlled if agriculture was to flourish. Harnessing the power of the Nile would also yield the hydroelectric power necessary for the increasingly industrial growth. Completed in 1902, its height was raised in subsequent building campaigns of 1907-12. The project was designed by Sir William Willcocks and involved several eminent engineers, including Sir John Aird whose firm, John Aird & Company, was the main contractor.

Sir Henry Royce, another patient recalled by Dr. Dent.

Sir John Aird was a regular visitor to Cromer. He was described by Dr. Dent as *quite an interesting personality with his keen face, long beard and complexion of remarkable high colour.* On one occasion when he was somewhat shabbily dressed Dr. Dent's maid mistook him for a Boer and bolted the front door in his face. In 1902 Sir John Aird hired Cromer Hall for the summer months. He repeated his visits to the area, hiring Hanworth Hall in 1903 and 1904.

In 1911 Mr. F.H. Royce, famed for Rolls-Royce motor cars, was suffering from a nervous breakdown and was under the care of Dr. Dent in Overstrand for three months. During this time his personal car was placed at Dr. Dent's disposal for especially long journeys into west Norfolk. Dr. Dent recorded:

It was sheer delight to travel in this car — Mr. Royce's own particular affection. There were no police traps in those days, and when moving at eighty miles an hour (on selected stretches of the practically untenanted roads of west Norfolk) no vibration whatever was to be noticed. What a record this wonderful man has established!

Royce, I believe, regards his engines as sentient things, for many a time when I have been in his room with him in Overstrand, I have noticed a look of real suffering pass over his features as he heard a maltreated engine protest when gear was changed by some neophyte of a driver in a passing car.

Situated immediately to the east of Sea Marge was a house known as Meadow Cottage. For some years this house was the summer retreat of Sir Frederick and Lady Macmillan. Frederick was the elder son of Daniel Macmillan who, with his brother Alexander, founded the publishing house of Macmillan in 1843. At the time Daniel was 30 and Alexander 25. Daniel suffered from ill health, leaving Alexander to take added responsibility for the running of the firm. He was a far sighted man and gave encouragement and responsibility to the second generation members of the firm, of whom Frederick was the oldest. During a stay of five years in America he learned the American book trade and married an American wife. By the time he was 37, *there was little in the whole range of the book trade that he had not already learned by hard work and personal experience.*[2] When Macmillan's became a limited company in 1896, Sir Frederick Macmillan became the first chairman. In the division of responsibility between his younger brother and his cousin, Frederick devoted himself in main to general literature. He was President of the Publishers Association 1900—1902.

In 1905 *The Times* newspaper started the Times Book Club. It served as a lending library for current books, but it soon became apparent *The Times* was in fact selling practically new books. The result was a bitter struggle between *The Times* and the book publishers. The details of that conflict are not relevant to the history of Poppyland. Suffice it to say that the dispute was not resolved until there was a new proprietor of *The Times* and that Sir Frederick Macmillan was largely responsible for bringing the dispute to an end. It was not for this, however, that he was knighted but for his work as Chairman of the Board of Management of the National Hospital for the Paralysed and Epileptic, Queen Square, London

Sir Frederick Macmillan was just as important a figure in the book trade as many other figures recorded in these pages were in their respective fields. Lady Battersea was a close friend of the Macmillans both in London and Overstrand. She wrote of them:

Sir Frederick Macmillan, the distinguished publisher, and his practical, clever little wife,[3] *inhabit during the summer months a charming*

cottage residence on the cliff, with a garden of small dimensions, but infinite variety and surprises. Sir Frederick, stout of build, ruddy of countenance, cheery of speech, delightful to meet, seems born to enjoy the good things of this life, amongst others the fine air of the Norfolk coast and the pleasant run of the golf links. I look upon the Macmillans as warm friends as well as valued neighbours.

Beyond Meadow Cottage was a property known as Cliffside. This summer residence belonged to Edward Boardman, the well known Norwich architect. Boardman was born in Norwich in 1833 and set up his own practice in Norwich in 1860. During a long and prolific career he did much work in Norwich in the private, ecclesiastical and public sectors. One of his major works was his sensitive conversion of Norwich Castle from a prison into a museum in 1887. It is said he interpreted accurately the archaeological remains, whilst at the same time creating a building admirably fitted for its new purpose. Considered by some to be his finest work is the impressively ornate Gothic mortuary temple that he designed in 1879 for the Rosary Cemetery in which he was later buried. Other well known Norwich landmarks for which he is remembered include rebuilding the Norwich and Norfolk Hospital, Alexandra Mansions in Prince of Wales Road, and the Royal Hotel in 1896–7 which he designed in a free Flemish style.

Edward Boardman undertook a number of commissions in Poppyland. As already mentioned, he designed the Overstrand Hotel. In Cromer he designed Carrington Villas, later known as Harbord House, 1878–79, on the Overstrand Road for Lord Suffield, in which Lord Suffield later lived. He designed the Fletcher Convalescent Home. He rebuilt the original Wesleyan Chapel dating from 1821 in 1881. This itself was replaced in 1910. In 1887 he rebuilt the Red Lion Hotel, adding an assembly room and stables.

Boardman's son, Edward Thomas Boardman (born 1862), joined the firm in 1889 and virtually took over after 1900 and carried on until 1966. He built the house at How Hill.

Mention was made earlier of The Grange built by Sir John Hare in 1901. It was sold to the cigarette mogul John Player in 1910. John Dane Player was the older of the two sons of John Player who first brought the firm of John Player and Sons of Nottingham into prominence. The two brothers became joint managing directors of the firm in 1895. The firm was noted for paying its workers high wages and for providing good working conditions. To John Player's generosity the village of Overstrand *was much indebted.*

However, John Player did not remain in Overstrand long. The Grange was subsequently purchased by the Reverend L.C. Carr, Rector of Overstrand, as a home for Mrs. Sarah Maria Wilson, who was the mother of Olive Carr, the rector's wife.

1   Compton McKenzie was the son of the actor Edward Compton, one of large family of actors of the surname McKenzie using Compton as a stage name. Fay Compton was his sister.
2   Charles Morgan, *The House of Macmillan* (London: Macmillan, 1943), p. 140.
3   She was a celebrated cook.

11

Celebrities 3: Politicians

When Cyril Flower was appointed Chief Whip in 1886 he commented to Constance, *it means real work and no hunting, no dinners and a great deal of London.* Surrey House, their London home, became a political meeting-ground for the Liberal party. From the earliest days of their marriage Cyril and Constance began entertaining their political allies and Liberal friends at their Surrey house. *A London house, with fine reception-rooms and a broad and easy staircase, was not to be despised at a time when the Liberal party demanded social functions,* wrote Lady Battersea later.

When they purchased their Cottage in Overstrand, it was not long before that, too, attracted Liberal politicians. One of their oldest political friends was John Morley, whom they had first met at Trent Park. He must have been one of the earliest celebrated politicians to stay in Overstrand when the Batterseas lent him their Cottage soon after its purchase. In the 1891 season he spent three months at his house, The Gables, Overstrand. This house was situated immediately to the west of the house later to be called Sea Marge, and was eventually incorporated into Sea Marge. Morley wrote:

> Our new house was spacious, standing open to sky and sea with a fine piece of meadow-land between us and the water, and excellent quarters for servants, who have well earned air and space after the dingy inferno of a London basement.[1]

It is believed this house was designed for John Morley by the architect Edward Boardman, who later lived just three doors down the road in an easterly direction. It was during this stay that the friendship between Cyril and Constance and John Morley was cemented. In 1914 John

Morley — by this time Viscount Morley — wrote:

The happiest days of my life were passed in the early times at the Pleasaunce, the delightful days of friendship, gaiety, reading, and talks of serious things.[2]

In his *Recollections* John Morley records the names of some of the *political confederates* who visited him at The Gables. These included Sir Arthur Acland, who was a noted Liberal politician and political author He is best remembered for his involvement with educational issues. The name of the philosopher and political theorist Herbert Spencer is also recorded. The mention of these names prompts the thought of how many more names of well known men and women who visited Poppyland are unrecorded.

John Morley was a towering strength in Liberal politics and English public life during his lifetime. He was a statesman, writer, man of letters, newspaper editor and distinguished political commentator. He has been called the *last of the great nineteenth century Liberals*. Among the positions he held in government were Chief Secretary of State for Ireland, Secretary of State for India and Lord President of the Council. Having been a Member of Parliament, he was raised to the Peerage as Viscount Blackburn in 1908. His influence stretched far beyond the field of politics. For many years he was a reader for the publishing house of Macmillan and close to the centre of policy making.[3]

From the earliest days of the events recorded above, there was a strong liberal and progressive influence prevailing in this area of Norfolk.. It was written of Samuel Hoare (I) that he was of the *most irreproachable integrity, always ready to assist and serve the poor, without regarding their religious sentiments.* This liberal tradition was exemplified by the third Lord Suffield, Sir Thomas Fowell Buxton and Elizabeth Fry. It continued with old Lady Hannah Buxton well into the nineteenth century who died at the age of 89 in 1872. This liberal influence came to fruition around the turn of the century when, in addition to Lord and Lady Battersea, three influential Liberal members of Parliament bought homes in the area.[4] One of these was Henry Fowler, who was recorded by John Morley *as* visiting The Gables in 1891 .

Henry Fowler began his political career in Wolverhampton where he served as a local councillor, becoming Mayor in 1866. In 1885 he was elected Member of Parliament for Wolverhampton East, retaining the

CELEBRITIES 3: POLITICIANS

eat until raised to the peerage as Viscount Wolverhampton in 1908. He held various offices of state under four Liberal Prime Ministers. Her served as Under-Secretary of State for the Home Department, 884-85, under Gladstone and as Secretary of State of India under Lord Rosebery. Under Sir Henry Campbell-Bannerman he served as Chancellor of the Duchy of Lancaster and under Asquith as Lord President of the Council. He was elected President of the Law Society, 1901–02. He was widely thought of as a future Prime Minister, but retired in 1910 owing to ill health. Henry Fowler had the distinction of being the first Methodist to become a government minister. He built the house known as Carrwood House, Carr Lane, Overstrand and was a friend of Lord and Lady Battersea. On his death in 1911, Carrwood House was left by Lord Wolverhampton to his son and two daughters. Lady Battersea wrote:

The father's intellectual capacities, although in a somewhat different line, have descended to the daughters. Both sisters are vivacious talkers, very entertaining, lively, and fully interested in the things of the day. They are remarkable for the quick repartee and brilliant epigrams, which follow one another in such succession that I find it difficult to give any adequate idea of their animated conversation. Carrwood House is a pleasant holiday home for both families.

The second of these three Liberal members of parliament was a man whose family had been embedded in the local community for many years. He was Sydney Charles Buxton. His father was Charles Buxton, the third son of Sir Thomas Fowell Buxton and Lady Hannah Gurney of Earlham, of Foxwarren, Cobham.

He entered Parliament in 1883 by winning a by-election in Peterborough, but was defeated in the 1885 general election. Buxton became prominent in political circles through the publication of his *Handbook to the Political Questions of the Day*. This was a series of 1/- books explaining to the general public in political, but non-party, terms, issues of the day that lay within the political arena.

He returned to Parliament in 1886, representing Poplar. During the course of his parliamentary career he served as Under-Secretary of State for the Colonies, Postmaster-General and President of the Board of Trade. In this last office he requested the Lord Chancellor to appoint a commission of enquiry into the sinking of the *Titanic*. In 1914 he was appointed Governor General of South Africa, and was created Viscount Buxton. Sydney Buxton was the owner of Shipbourne, Vicarage Road, Cromer.

Situated in Overstrand churchyard near the road and west of the church tower, is a large granite monument. The inscription reads:

> TO THE GLORY OF GOD AND IN MEMORY OF ELIZA WIFE
> OF HENRY BROADHURST, J.P. BORN 17th DEC, 1834, DIED
> 24th MAY 1905. ...ALSO OF HENRY BROADHURST BORN
> 13th APRIL 1840 DIED 11th OCT 1911 ... HE WAS A MEMBER
> OF PARLIAMENT FOR 25 YEARS; UNDER HOME SECRETARY
> OF STATE IN 1886; SECRETARY OF THE TRADES UNION
> CONGRESS FROM 1875 TO 1890; ALDERMAN AND J.P. FOR
> NORFOLK. HE FOUGHT A GOOD FIGHT AND CHAMPIONED
> THE CAUSE OF THE POOR, THE TOILERS AND THE
> OPPRESSED.

The most unusual of these three Liberal Members of Parliament with homes in Poppyland was Henry Broadhurst. The outline of his achievements is recorded on his tombstone above. However, these achievements are all the more remarkable when his humble background is considered. Henry Broadhurst was born at Littlemore, Oxfordshire, the eleventh or twelfth child of a large family. He left school at the age of twelve, working first for a local blacksmith, later training as a stonemason. Small beginnings in the Trade Union movement led him being appointed secretary to the Trades Union Parliamentary Committee. He became involved in many contemporary social issues, including the struggle for universal suffrage. In the 1880 general election he was elected as Liberal member of parliament for Stoke-on-Trent.

In the 1885 General Election Henry Broadhurst was elected Member of Parliament for the Bordesley Division of Birmingham. In February, 1886, he received the following letter from the Prime Minister:

Dear Mr Broadhurst,-

I have very great pleasure in proposing to you that you should accept office as Under-Secretary of State in the Home Department. Alike on private and on public grounds I trust it may be acceptable to you to accept this appointment, which should remain strictly secret until your name has been before Her Majesty.

I remain, with much regard,
Sincerely Yours,
W.E. Gladstone.

On receipt of this letter Broadhurst mused upon his past life:

Like a drowning man, I lived my life over again in the next half-hour. The lowly beginning of my career, its labours at the forge and stonemason's shop, the privations, the wanderings, and my varying fortunes, stood out in my mind's eye as clearly as so many living pictures. Especially did my memory recall the months I had spent working on the very Government buildings which I was about to enter as a Minister of the Crown.

Henry Broadhurst, like Henry Fowler, broke new ground in his political career. He was the first man from a working class background to become a Minister of the Crown. At the Royal Cromer Golf Club he met Arthur Balfour. The contrast between the two was complete: Balfour educated at Eton and Christ Church, Oxford; Broadhurst leaving school at twelve and once working on the chimneys of Christ Church as a stonemason; one an aristocrat, the other a man of the people; one reserved, the other hale and 'well met'. It is hardly surprising they had their differences.

On one occasion Balfour arrived unexpectedly to play golf at Cromer. He was greeted by the bluff Harry Broadhurst with the words, *Glad to see you Mr. Balfour. You've come down for a little game of golf, 'ave you?* Balfour replied, *Yes, you surely do not think I had journeyed all this long way from town for the special purpose of speaking to you?*

Balfour and Broadhurst also clashed in the House of Commons:

Decidedly the best part of yesterday morning's debate on the Education Bill was Mr. Broadhurst's 'Excursion to Cromer.' It was an excursion only in the mind's eye, but it captivated the House; and one could see from Mr. Broadhurst's rosy countenance, puckered with smiles, that he was very pleased — as they say in the country — to give the tired legislators this little treat. It seemed at first rather hard to get a vision of Poppyland with heather springing turf and the roar of the sea 'spatchcocked' into a debate on the Education Bill; but Mr. Broadhurst, who is a master-craftsman in his way, did it.

Mr. Broadhurst decanted on Cromer as a place of 'worldwide renown'; and gradually worked up to an argument that people who were so fortunate as to live there ought to be allowed to manage their own school affairs. The appeal was so quaint and fetching that even Mr. Balfour — at one in the morning — was softened to make a special reply as 'the case of Cromer', insidiously attacking Mr. Broadhurst's defence by putting in 'a good word for the Norfolk County Council'.

However, despite their differences, Broadhurst asked Balfour to write the Introduction to his autobiography. Balfour paid him the following compliment:

Here is Mr. Broadhurst, who stands four-square to all the winds that blow, who has earned his own living since he was twelve years old, who got married at nineteen, who knows all the mysteries of the forge and has wrought in stone, who has faced with ready wit and determined aspect every kind of audience, big, little, and respectable, friendly, false, and furious, in almost every town of great Britain, who has defended his character from calumnious assaults, frontal, side, and secret, who has drafted reports, framed resolutions, considered amendments, and made play with statistics, who has piloted bills through all their stages in the House of Commons, who has spoken on innumerable occasions in that difficult Assembly, from both front benches and back, above the gangway and below it, who has been greeted with every kind of cheer, not excepting the ironical, who has known both failure and success, what it is to win and lose an election, to be in and out of parliament.

In his autobiography Henry Broadhurst recalls his friendship with Edward, Prince of Wales, which came about through his membership of the 1884 Royal Commission on the Housing of the Working Classes of which the Prince was a member. The Prince invited the whole Commission to visit the Sandringham estate. Broadhurst was unable to accept, but went on a subsequent occasion.

I spent three days at Sandringham with the Prince and Princess, and I can honestly say that I was never entertained more to my liking and never felt more at home when paying a visit than I did on this occasion.[5]

Henry Broadhurst recorded another incident connected with the Prince in 1889, when in his own words *I founded the Cromer Golf Club. His Royal Highness, in response to my invitation, consented to act as patron and gave the first prize, a handsome silver bowl.[6]*

The Broadhursts, probably photographed in the garden of their home at Trent Cottage.

Henry Broadhurst lived the latter years of his life at Trent Cottage, now Trent House. It was situated on the Overstrand Road just below the Royal Cromer Golf Club, which at one time was in the parish of Overstrand.

Three British Prime Ministers holding office consecutively in the first decade of the twentieth century patronized Poppyland, though not necessarily while in office. The first of these was Arthur Balfour. He succeeded his uncle, Lord Salisbury, as Prime Minister in 1896. Balfour enjoyed playing tennis at New Haven Court with Locker-Lampson. He developed a *consuming passion* for golf. When not in office he endeavoured to play a round every day. He played at Cromer with Sir Samuel Hoare. As nephew of Lord Salisbury Balfour was at the heart of the British establishment. He and Lord Curzon were the acknowledged male leaders of that privileged and aristocratic group friends known as the *Souls*. When Curzon was appointed Viceroy of India of India in 1898, he gave a celebrated dinner party at the Hotel Cecil, London, on 9th December. Each guest found in their place at table a few lines describing their character. Of Balfour, Curzon wrote:

There was to be seen at that feast
Of this band, the High Priest,
The heart that to all hearts is nearest.;
Him may nobody steal
From the true common weal,
Tho' to each is dear, Arthur the dearest.

When Arthur Balfour was forced into resignation in 1906, he was replaced as Prime Minister by the Liberal Sir Henry Campbell-Bannerman, who won a sweeping victory in the general election of that year. Dr. Dent recorded meeting him at New Haven Court as a cabinet minister. Following the 1910 general election, the Liberals also formed the next government. Campbell-Bannerman resigned shortly afterwards through illness, and Herbert Henry Asquith become Prime Minister. Asquith had a long association with Poppyland, which began soon after the Batterseas purchased the Pleasaunce.

> *Strolling on the Cromer cliffs a few evenings ago, I came upon an interesting Parliamentary apparition in the form of Mr. Herbert Henry Asquith, Secretary of State for the Home Department, resplendent in a light tweed coat, a pair of flannel 'continuations', and a golf cap. I doubt if a Cabinet Minister has ever been encountered in a more airy or jaunty costume. Thus arrayed in all his holiday glory, the Home Secretary look more boyish than ever, and it was almost impossible to believe that he could ever have sat at solemn Downing Street conclaves, and considered petitions for the reprieve of criminals condemned to suffer the last penalty of the law. Mr. Asquith had run down for a day or two as the guest of Lord Battersea, whose charming retreat at Overstrand is ever open to his over-worked friends of all shades. The erstwhile Liberal whip seems to cherish the laudable idea of making his 'Pleasaunce' into a Parliamentary sanatorium, and there will be few prominent politicians to whom he has not revealed the beauties of his Poppyland House.[7]*

In 1901 Asquith and his second wife, Margot, paid several weekend visits to Cromer. Margot was the youngest of the four daughters of the Scottish industrialist Sir Charles Tennant. They were high spirited and unconventional girls. Margot's entry into London society was compared to an assault. It can well be argued that Margot Asquith was the most dynamic celebrity of all the many to visit Poppyland. She was often called an *electric charge* at a party. *All her life Margot was in the headlines: every exploit, every flirtation audacious, every bon mot was pounced on by the press.* In 1893 she performed a skirt dance at the *Folies Bergères* and overnight became the rage of Paris. She was drawn by Toulouse-Lautrec. She was sculptured as an electric light and it is said she inspired the curves on the buildings of the new Metro. She was immortalised by E.F. Benson in his novel, *Dodo*.

Dr. Dent drew a thumbnail sketch of her in Cromer:

> *More than once in 1901, I saw Margot standing upright in one of those antique two-seaters [a springless donkey chair] and laying on with*

hearty goodwill to a sullen donkey, while Asquith reclined with folded
arms, apparently wholly unconscious of the humour of the situation.

One can just imagine the scene: Margot, quite unselfconsciously
aying into this donkey, oblivious of everything around. Thus the
rrepressible Margot Asquith found her match in form of a recalcitrant
Cromer donkey.

Members of the Churchill family had associations with Poppyland
hroughout the time covered by this book. In 1885 Lady Randoph
Churchill brought her sons Winston and his younger brother to Cromer
or August and September. They were patients of Dr. Fenner. On one
occasion he was for sent for by a lady who was in charge of the two boys.
Winston, then a boy of eleven, in a childish fit of temper had thrown an
nk pot at her with damaging effect. Dr. Fenner then led young Winston
upstairs and took an active part in making the *punishment fit the crime.*
n 1909 Consuelo, Duchess of Marlborough brought her two sons, the
Marquis of Blandford and Lord Ivor Churchill to Cromer. They stayed on
Western Parade near the Grand Hotel. When Dr. Dent had occasion to
treat the two boys he told them of the incident with the young Winston.
The next day the two boys produced letters they had both written to
Winston, commencing: *Dear Cousin Winston, we have the same doctors*
who spanked you for throwing an ink-pot at your nurse. Lady Randoph
Churchill was a frequent visitor to Overstrand up to the time of the Great
War and was often to be met either at the Danish Pavilion or Sea Marge

In 1913 Winston and Clementine Churchill landed at Cromer from the
admiralty yacht *Enchantress.* It was a breezy day and while disembarking
n a small boat Clementine's dress became badly damaged by the salt
water. Later that day Dr. Dent recalled that he met the Churchills at New
Haven Court with no one present but Jane and Commander Oliver
Locker-Lampson. Clementine complained to Dr. Dent about the absence
of a landing-stage.

Dr. Dent recorded:

She was much amused when I told her it was entirely her husband's
fault, because I well knew as one of the Protection Commissioners that
application had been made to the Admiralty months previously for
Government monetary support for a landing stage, on plea that naval
units were constantly calling at Cromer. I told her that the Admiralty

Overstrand beach, where Winston Churchill and his family spent time in the summer of 1914, prior to the outbreak of war.

acknowledged   our   letter expressing regret that they were unable to promise any assistance.

Mrs Churchill turned to her husband, who had been First Lord of the Admiralty since 1911. He merely gave a non-committal smile. There was no telephone at Pear Tree Cottage. Sir Edgar and Lady Speyer kindly lent Clementine the use of their telephone at Sea Marge at pre-set times for the Churchills to keep in touch.

War on Germany was declared on 4th August. It has been asserted that as First Lord of the Admiralty, Winston Churchill despatched the telegram mobilising the fleet from Sea Marge. This may be so, but in her war diaries Margot Asquith recounts being in the Cabinet Room, 10, Downing Street, at the hour war was declared with the Prime Minister, Reginald McKenna, the Home Secretary and Lord Grey, Foreign Secretary:

Big Ben struck 11: Boom, Boom, Boom. We all sat in complete silence I should say for 10 minutes after the last Boom. Winston dashed into the room radiant — his face bright, his manner keen, and he told us, one word pouring out on the other, how he was going to send telegrams to the Mediterranean! the North Sea and God knows where.[8]

1   John Morley, *Recollections*, vol. 1 (London: Macmillan, 1917), p. 271
2   Constance Battersea, *Reminiscences* (London: Macmillan, 1922), p. 173.
3   For a fuller account of Morley's influence at Macmillans see Charles Morgan, *The House of Macmillan* (London: Macmillan, 1943), chapter 7.
4   I am indebted to Mr. G. Kidd for pointing this out.
5   *Henry Broadhurst, Henry Broadhurst, M.P.: The story of his life from a stonemason's bench to the Treasury bench* (London: Hutchinson, 1901), p. 150.
6   Broadhurst, p. 156.
7   *The Lancaster Gazette*, September 1893.
8   Margot Asquith, *Margot Asquith's Great War Diary, 1914—1916: the view from Downing Street* ed. Michael and Eleanor Brock (Oxford: Oxford University Press, 2014), p. 108.

12

Four Second Homes

Overstrand must possess some potent charm, since so many visitors who come but for a short holiday and end by purchasing, or trying to purchase, a small pied-a-terre on this coast.

So wrote Lady Battersea.[1] Compared to the Pleasaunce, Lady Battersea's Overstrand home, no doubt these second homes did appear small. These were, however, substantial houses and helped to give Overstrand its soubriquet 'the millionaire's village'.

Corner Cottage, Paul's Lane, Overstrand

A house in Overstrand, now of peculiar excrescent shape, owing to the successive additions made to the previous structure by its various interesting occupants, stands but a stone's throw from the Danish Pavilion across the road. When I first knew it in 1888 it was known as 'Dr. Beverley's Cottage,' to which the owner came for a short holiday from Norwich when pressure of professional work demanded relaxation. Dr. Beverley was for many years the doyen of the medical profession in Norwich, where he had a large general practice, and whose services as a consulting physician were in great request all over the County.

With these words Dr. Dent described the house known then as Corner Cottage, situated on a blind corner in Pauls Lane, Overstrand.[2] In 1891 Dr. Beverley was living at 54, Prince of Wales Road, Norwich. Corner Cottage was part of the Manor of Overstrand. It was enfranchised in 1901. The plan on the enfranchisement shows it as two separate buildings, the southern part being residential, while the northern was designated agricultural use. In October, 1906, it was purchased by the Dowager Countess of Yarborough, who had married in 1881 as her second husband John Maunsell Richardson. Richardson and Cyril Flower were old university friends. Cyril and Constance Flower visited the Countess at Brocklesbury Hall, Lincolnshire, in 1878 when Constance met Richardson for the first time. At Corner Cottage *A transformation scene under my husband's auspices soon took place*, wrote Lady Battersea. The cottage assumed the look of a villa and was renamed Corner House. She commented: *On many occasions he and his wife, Lady Yarborough, were our guests in our Norfolk home, and as our North-east Coast appealed more and more to them both.*

With the coming of the Countess of Yarborough, history turned full circle. She was the granddaughter of Admiral Lukin, later Windham, of Felbrigg Hall by his daughter Maria Augusta, who married first George Wyndham of Cromer Hall and, secondly, the Earl of Listowel. Their daughter, Victoria Alexandrina Hare, married Charles Anderson-Pelham, third Earl of Yarborough, of Brocklesbury Hall, north Lincolnshire when she was eighteen. Her coming into north Lincolnshire *caused a revolution of the most joyous kind over the whole countryside.[3]* She *completely captivated* all who knew her. *She was simply adored in Lincolnshire,[4]* both for her warmth of character and for her prowess in the hunting field. She was one of the finest, if not the finest, horse-woman of her age.

However, the Earl of Yarborough died on 6th February 1875, aged 40. The widowed Countess continued living at Brocklesbury Hall and managing the estate. She *took the horn* to the Brocklesbury hounds, becoming one of only two women Masters'of Fox Hounds in the nineteenth century, the other being Lady Salisbury. She

The Countess of Yarborough and John Maunsell Richardson,1911, who owned Corner Cottage, Pauls Lane, Overstrand 1906-1912, The Countess was Admiral Lukin's grand-daughter.

waited until her son attained his coming of age in 1880 and the following year married the man of her choice and near neighbour and long term friend, John Maunsell Richardson, who had been assisting her since the Earl's death. He was five years younger than the Countess and had long admired her from a distance.

John Maunsell Richard Richardson was England's most celebrated amateur jockey. While at Harrow he acquired the nickname of 'Cat', which stuck to him for the rest of his life. On leaving Harrow, he went up to Magdalene College, Cambridge. He took up residence not in the college buildings but at French's, the well-known lodging house by Park Street, Jesus Lane.

French's, which was the recognised headquarters of the *crème de la crème*, so to speak, of the sporting set at Cambridge, was a most exclusive establishment and exceedingly difficult to get into, every one desirous of becoming a member having to be proposed and seconded just the same as at a club.[5]

As an undergraduate he achieved the prestigious position of Master of the University Drag Hounds and it was at Cambridge, and still in his teens, that his career in steeplechasing began in earnest. In 1865 the Cat won his first public steeplechase at Huntingdon his own mare Vienna. Seven years later in 1872 he eclipsed all his previous performances, winning no less than fifty-six events, four of which were on the flat. *It was a singular incident that of the four races under Jockey Club Rules he rode in that year at Epsom and Liverpool he should win them all.*

The Cat's career in racing culminated in the years 1873 and 1874 when he won the Grand National Steeplechase on both occasions. In 1873 he won on the six year old Disturbance, beating a field of 26 runners at the odds of 16/1. In 1874 he won on the six year old Reugny beating a field of 21 runners at the odds of 5/1. Both horses belonged to the doyen of steeplechasing, Captain Machel, for whom Richardson had been riding. The latter proved to be the Cat's last race. It resulted in a bitter dispute with Captain Machell and the Cat retired from racing.

On retirement from racing he continued taking an active part in many aspects of country life and sports, especially hunting. He was much in demand as a judge at horse shows. In 1900 the Countess and the Cat left Lincolnshire and settled at Edmondthorpe, Rutlandshire, where the Cat became joint master of the Cottesmore Hunt. When they bought

Corner House, Overstrand, he joined Royal Cromer Golf Club. He excelled at ball games and mastered golf to such an extent that towards the end of his life he was elected President of the club. The beginning of John Maunsell's last illness began on Cromer golf course when on completing *two well contested rounds of golf* he developed a serious attack of influenza. Although well enough to travel back to Edmondthorpe, and even to hunt occasionally, his health had been impaired. He died on 22nd January, 1912, aged 65 years.

The funeral took place in Edmondthorpe parish church.

> *All through the service it seemed as if one great sob went out from each heart, not only for her who had sustained the greatest loss of all, but for themselves. Then as the bier was conveyed to the graveside, as if by one impulse, the whole congregation turned towards it, and so they took farewell to their friend.*[6]

As the coffin was lowered into the ground a few snowflakes fell. Lady Battersea paid this tribute to him:

> *Everywhere he was a favourite both with young and old, with men of culture, men of business, agriculturalists, the Norfolk fishermen and those of sporting tastes. He had the qualities of a true English gentleman. His respect for women and children was most beautiful, and as his trim and compact figure might have been seen Sunday after Sunday, wending its way churchwards, always accompanied by that ever-constant and inimitable companion, his wife, I felt that amongst the congregation there could not have a heart more faithful to its early teaching, humbler in self-appreciation or more grateful for a life rich friendship and in home affections.*[7]

On the death of her husband the Countess sold Corner House to the Reverend Charles Barclay in October, 1912. His wife, Florence, like other of the women and men who visited Poppyland in its prime, and whose names will be familiar to only a minority today, achieved international fame. Her life, which began conventionally for its age, was far from conventional. This was due to her exceptional physical, spiritual and literary powers.

Her father was Vicar of Limpsfield, Surrey, and later of St. Anne's, Limehouse. From him she learned a deep personal love of God and a

onviction of the inspiration of the Holy Scriptures, which never left
1er. As a girl she was precocious, confident and unselfconscious. She
vas exceptionally musical. At the age of four she had developed a fine
:ontralto voice. At the age of nine she was asked to lead the singing
vhen the service had to be held in the Town Hall while the church was
undergoing repairs. Her mother quickly came to rely on her and she
vas engaged in parish work from an early age. At the age of eighteen she
married the Reverend Charles Barclay of Bury Hill, Surrey, by whom she
1ad eight children. He had been her father's curate in Limehouse and
vas later appointed to the living of Hatfield Heath, Hertfordshire.

It was a natural extension of her former work that she should assist
1er husband in parish work. Her Bible classes for women were so well
prepared and appreciated that their fame spread. In 1913 she packed the
Free Trade Hall, Manchester, with an enthusiastic audience of 3,500 for
1er talk on 'The Inspiration of the Bible'. Her younger sister was married
o Ballington Booth who was the son of 'General' Booth, the founder of
.he Salvation Army, and founded the Volunteers of America. In 1909
Florence visited America to accompany her sister on a Chautauqua
:our.[8] She covered 7,000 miles in three weeks, speaking to audiences of
anything between 2,500 and 5,000, and once to 8,000.

Florence was physically athletic and excelled in many sports and
enjoyed bicycling. In 1905 she bicycled from Hatfield to Cromer in a
day. This long ride over-strained her heart. She was forced to lie flat and
endure painful attacks. Previously she had completed for no particular
reason a little story entitled The Wheels of Time. She showed it to her sister
n America who recognised its worth and insisted on its publication,
which took place in 1908.

This in turn led to her novel The Rosary which was published
simultaneously in London and America in November, 1909. By the
end of the first year 150,000 copies had been sold and for a time two
impressions a month were being printed. Sales eventually topped the
one million mark. The novel was translated into eight languages. The
title had become a household word. The book was to be seen everywhere.

By the time her husband had purchased Corner House Florence
Barclay was a well established novelist. She came to love her country
retreat in Overstrand where she continued her writing, both there and in
the sunken garden at the Pleasaunce, by the invitation of Lady Battersea.

Florence Barclay had long admired the love story of Robert and Elizabeth Browning. On Robert Browning's death she bought a number of effects from his sale including his arm chair, which she placed in her writing room at Corner House. This became known as the *Browning Room*. Her writing desk is still *in situ*. However, her busy life had taken its toll on her health. She died in 1921, aged 58 years, after deteriorating health.

New Haven Court, Cromer

Frederick Locker, later of New Haven Court, Cromer, was born in 1821 at Greenwich where his father was Civil Commissioner for Greenwich Hospital. His grandfather was Admiral William Locker, much loved by Lord Nelson for his advice *lay a Frenchman close, and you will beat him*. Young Frederick showed little aptitude for work and was given a desultory education. Almost as a last resort he began his working life as a colonial clerk in Mincing Lane, London. Possibly through his naval connection, Lord Minto, First Lord of the Admiralty, gave Locker a temporary clerkship at Somerset House. Later he was transferred to Lord Haddington's private office where he rose to be deputy reader to the assembled Board. It was his responsibility to read the principal despatches, decipher telegrams, to act on his own judgement and if necessary contact the relevant cabinet minister. He *kept a folio book, posted up to the hour, which showed the station of every ship in the navy.* While Locker was a clerk at the Admiralty, Anthony Trollope was a clerk at the Post Office. The two were excellent friends and exchanged many letters. In 1849, finding himself suffering from what he called *acute nervous depression*, he took leave of absence from work. In July, 1850, he married Lady Charlotte Bruce, the daughter of Lord Elgin who had brought the Parthenon marbles to London. The marriage produced one daughter.

Lady Charlotte Bruce was well liked by Queen Victoria. Her brother was Colonel Robert Bruce, whom the Prince Consort placed in charge of the Prince of Wales during a educational visit to Italy in January, 1859. As a Major General he was placed in charge of the Prince when he was an under-graduate at Oxford University later in the year. Lady Charlotte's sister was Lady Augusta Bruce, who was Queen Victoria's favourite Lady in Waiting, who *always answered 'Yes, ma'am to everything she* [the Queen] *said and was promoted to a privileged permanent position at her side.*[9] She married the Very Reverend Arthur Stanley, Dean of Westminster Abbey, another favourite of the Queen.

Frederick Locker was a man of delicacy and taste.

He sometimes seemed to me to be all taste. Whatever subject he approached — was it the mystery of religion, or the moralities of life, a poem or a print, a bit of old china or a human being — whatever it might be, it was along the avenue of taste that he gently made his way up to it.[10]

Even stronger, however, than his taste, was his love of kindness. He was too gentle a person to have the ruthlessness to rise to the top of a profession, but he was born with an innate capacity for friendship.

He had friends everywhere, in all ranks of life, who found in him an infinity of solace and for his friends there was nothing he would not do. It seemed as if he could not spare himself.

He wrote of himself:

The observation of my fellow-creatures — their fancies, their peculiarities, their virtues, and their foibles — has almost unconsciously to myself been one of my favourite diversions in life, and one of the most remunerative, for I do not like my species the worse for it; but it has taught me to live comfortably with mankind and must not expect too much from them.[11]

Locker had a deep love of poetry and of books. In 1857 he published a slim volume of poetry entitled *London Lyrics*. Locker was not a great poet, but neither was he a poor poet. His poems are beautifully crafted and reflect his observations on life. Other slim volumes followed. He corresponded with many of the leading poets of the day, including Alfred Tennyson, to whom he sent a copy of *London Lyrics*. Tennyson replied on 1st February, 1858.

Sir,

Thanks for your clever little book. I have such reams of verses to acknowledge that I cannot even get through the work of thanking authors for them. A furious letter from one whom I had neglected so alarmed me just now that I dared not put off acknowledging your book any longer — but I had read your book otherwise I should not have called it clever. Now, here are twenty more to answer.

Farewell, Yours
A. TENNYSON
(In the eighth year of my persecution)[12]

Frederick Locker became a close friend of the Tennyson family. He stayed with them at Farringford House, Isle of Wight. In May, 1865, Lady Tennyson recorded in her journal: *Mr. Locker leaves. We have had long walks. Very kind & pleasant he has been.* In later life Alfred Tennyson was a not infrequent visitor to New Haven Court. He and Locker travelled in Europe together. Tennyson is recorded as an old man walking across Cromer golf links. Locker's daughter, Eleanor, married Tennyson's son, Lionel. He died aged 30. She married secondly the Hon. Augustus Birrell.

Lady Charlotte Locker died in 1872. In 1878 Locker married the younger Jane Lampson, daughter of Sir Curtis Lampson who was born at New Haven, Vermont, U.S.A, after which New Haven Court was possibly named. He was involved in laying the first transatlantic cable. Subsequently he became a British citizen. When created a Baronet in 1866, he is thought to have been the first American born citizen to be so honoured. Following his death in 1895, Frederick Locker added the name Lampson to Locker, thus becoming the more familiar Frederick Locker-Lampson.

Today, as the traveller leaves Cromer on the Norwich road, passing the traffic lights guarding the Overstrand Road, the road begins to rise. The third turning on the right is known today as Court Drive. It leads up an incline the full extent of which is obscured by bungalows lining either side of the road. From the top of this wind- swept location there is a commanding view of Cromer and over the sea. It was on this site in 1884 that Jane Lampson built New Haven Court under the guidance of her father. Frederick Locker wrote a none-too-flattering verse about it:

This is the house by Cromer town,
Its bricks are red, though they look so brown,
It faces the sea on a wind-swept hill —
In winter its empty, in summer it's chill
Indeed it is one of Earth's windiest spots
As we know from the crashing of chimney-pots.
This is the house that Jane built.[13]

Frederick Locker had created a wide circle of friends in all walks of life from his varied activities and interests, many of whom were entertained at Cromer. In his *Reminiscences* Dr. Dent paid tribute to the friendliness of Locker-Lampson on his arrival as the assistant to Dr. Fenner, the Cromer doctor, in 1889:

> *It is not too much to say that it was the kindly welcome and encouragement given to me by Frederick Locker-Lampson in those early days of my Cromer life, which more than anything else helped to drive away introspection and depression of spirits.*

New Haven Court at Cromer. 'It faces the sea on a windswept hill.'

New Haven Court was the centre of intellectual and social life of Cromer at this time. The English poet and essayist Henry Austin Dobson wrote in the visitor's book:

> Cromer in Norfolk's a pleasant resort,
> And the best thing in Cromer is New Haven Court.

Among the many guests entertained at New Haven Court there was usually a preponderance of literary figures. Frederick Locker-Lampson was not greatly interested in politics, but he took a delight in bringing together guests of differing opinions. On one celebrated occasion a foursome at tennis consisted of Arthur Balfour and William Scawen

Blunt on one side and Lord Houghton (later Marquis of Crewe) and Dr. Dent on the other. Only a few months previously Lord Houghton, then Chief Secretary for Ireland, and Arthur Balfour had imprisoned Blunt over the O'Brien affair. The children's book illustrator Kate Greenaway was a regular visitor to New Haven. Dr. Dent recalled meeting Oscar Wilde there.

Locker-Lampson died in 1895 and is buried at Worth near Rowfont, the home of Sir Curtis Lampson, the main residence of Frederick and Jane. On her husband's death Jane Locker-Lampson continued spending time at New Haven Court. Among the guests was the explorer, Ernest Shackleton. In 1909 Shackleton gave a lecture to the Cromer Conservative Club. (The Club had opened four years previously.) The Club presented Shackleton with a specially commissioned pair of gold cuff links, with a white enamel circle and a blue enamel centre. The gold symbolised the *sterling qualities of bravery* of Shackleton's forthcoming Antarctic Expedition, the white enamel the Antarctic wastes, and the blue symbolised Cromer's sky and sea. There is an extant photograph which shows Mr. and Mrs. Shackleton,

The explore Ernest Shackleton and Mrs Shackleton standing outside New Haven Court. In the centre is Lady Battersea.

he Vicar of Cromer, Jane and
Oliver Locker-Lampson and
Lady Battersea standing in
front of New Haven Court.

Long after the end of the
1914—1918 war, and past
the scope of this book, New
Haven Court was a centre
of social life in Cromer. It
boasted some of the finest
tennis courts in England.
Many celebrated tournaments
were played there. Josephine
Brown, now nearing ninety,
attended a small private school
in Cliff Avenue, Cromer, and

*The indoor courts at Newhaven Court.
Samuel Hoare's 'damn' at a fault and
'double damn' at a double fault was long
remembered by a young lady who acted
as 'ball-boy' there.*

well remembers the sense of importance in attending ballet classes in
the dance hall there.

Later in its life, New Haven Court became a hotel. The end came
in the exceptionally cold winter of 1962—63. After a disastrous fire in
which the firemen had to break the ice on the fire hydrants with a sledge
hammer, the building was badly damaged. The ruins were never rebuilt
and a block of flats eventually appeared on the site.

Danish House, Overstrand

In 1900 France staged the Paris Exhibition to celebrate the achievements
of the past century and accelerate developments in the new. The style of
the exhibits was *Art Nouveau*. More than fifty million people attended
the exhibition, including Lady Elizabeth Lewis, wife of Sir George Lewis,
the celebrated lawyer. On the Quay d'Orsay along the River Seine in the
Rue des Nations were eight pavilions reflecting the architectural styles
of their respective countries of origin, including Denmark. Lady Lewis
so admired the Danish Pavilion that Sir George bought the pavilion
and had it re-erected on a site in Pauls Lane, Overstrand, known today
as Danish House Gardens, under the supervision of the of Norwich
architects Edward Boardman and Son. Additional living space, a stable
block and servants' quarters were added.

The shape of the whole completed complex can be compared to a capital letter U on its side. The closed loop of the U, facing in a westerly direction, consisted of the servants' quarters. At right angles to it, the southern arm was the stable block. These were not as high as the actual Pavilion. The two open arms of the U were joined by a covered walkway, facing in an easterly direction. On approaching the site from Pauls Lane, a visitor would skirt the stables, enter the covered walkway, turn right and so approach the actual Pavilion itself, which formed the northern arm of the U. This gave it an uninterrupted view over the sea. The extensive grounds were landscaped and there was a path leading to the cliff top. Below, the beach was known as Lady Lewis's beach.

George Lewis was the one solicitor whose name became a household word. He sported an eyeglass, grew Dundreary whiskers and whatever the weather wore a thick fur coat. These were as famous as Mr. Gladstone's collar or Mr. Chamberlain's orchid. When he attended the opening night of *Trial by Jury*, W.S. Gilbert played a public joke on him. The actor playing the solicitor was made-up to look exactly like George Lewis with the familiar monocle, Dundreary whiskers and fur coat. The audience loved it. As the applause swelled around them, Sir George and Lady Lewis pretended to be unmoved, but they must have appreciated the fact that Sir George was now recognised as a celebrity. For over twenty-five years he had the monopoly of cases where the seamy side of society unveiled the sins and follies of the wealthy and famous and threatened disaster if exposed.

George Lewis was born on 21st April, 1833. His father, James Lewis, had set up as a solicitor at 12, Ely Place, in the same year. The following year the firm became Lewis and Lewis when Charles took his brother into partnership. James Lewis was a successful and highly respected solicitor, noted for his generosity. He knew all the theatrical celebrities of the day, many of whom were his clients. Charles Keene played with young George Lewis on his knee. George kept up this association and interest in the theatre.

In 1847 Lewis went to University College, London. Three years later in 1850, at the age of seventeen and a-half he was articled to his father. Criminality was rife in London, where large areas were enclaves of crime. Lewis and Lewis specialised in criminal law. Perpetrators of petty crimes and not so petty crimes all came to Ely Place seeking the help of James

Lewis. This was the world that faced George Lewis when he finished his articles and became a solicitor in 1856 in his father's firm.

George Lewis was quickly recognised as a brilliant cross-examiner, with the capacity to get to the heart of a case, however complicated. His key to success was his meticulous thoroughness in his preparation. Every aspect of the case was examined and every detail of a witness's statement questioned. This thoroughness extended to his extensive use of a network of spies and informers, some of whom were ex-convicts. These were once described as *a spider's web of narks and informers* by someone less than enthusiastic about their existence. These gifts, coupled with an intense desire to win, whatever the merits of the client, made him a formidable adversary and won him enemies, as well as friends. In 1858 he was taken into partnership with his father.

In 1863 George Lewis married the gentle Victorine Kann, daughter of a German banker and merchant from Frankfurt-am-Main. Tragically, she died soon after giving birth to their daughter in April, 1865. He married secondly in 1867 Elizabeth Eberstadt, the youngest of the four beautiful of daughters Ferdinand Eberstadt of Mannheim, Germany. Beautiful as she was, it has been written *her intelligence transcended her beauty*, giving her the poise and self-possession to make her a celebrated hostess. When George and Elizabeth moved to 88, Portland Place in 1876 she turned it into a house filled with painters, sculptors, musicians, politicians and actors. *At the George Lewises one was quite sure to meet many amusing and interesting people.*[14] Among these were Edward and Mrs. Burne-Jones, George and Emma du Maurier, John Singer Sargent, James Whistler, Robert Browning, Henry James, Oscar Wilde, Henry Irving, Ellen Terry and Lillie Langtry. At his New Year parties, his actor friends took part in highly professionally acted charades. When George Lewis married Elizabeth Eberstadt he was *a lawyer with a successful criminal practice; when he died he was the lawyer of London.*[15]

During the course of his long career as a solicitor, George Lewis was involved in many of the most celebrated cases of fraud, murder, divorce, black mail and even prostitution, that came before the courts and that caught the popular imagination. In 1864 he was involved in a case that has remained unique in British criminals annals to this day, when a prisoner gave evidence against another for a murder for which he himself was under sentence of death.

Pauls Lane, Overstrand, looking west, c.1905. The Danish pavilion, with added staff accommodation and stables, can been on the right. The front is seen in the inset photo.

One famous case in which he took great interest as a lawyer, as did the journalist George R. Sims, was the flagrant miscarriage of justice in a case of mistaken identity. The Beck case was one of the worst cases of Home Office intransigence in British legal history. Lewis with his powerful influence in legal circles and Sims, equally powerful in the journalistic field, pressed for an official enquiry. The government gave in. At the enquiry, Lewis represented Adolf Beck. This enquiry was *largely instrumental* in bringing about the creation of the Court of Criminal Appeal, which had power to quash previous convictions. Lewis had long believed in the right of a prisoner to give evidence on his own behalf and the establishment of such a court.

When her jewels were stolen from a London bank Lillie Langtry at once appealed to George Lewis for help. She left this description of him:

A solicitor, as his father had been before him, he specialised in cases dealing with the seamy side of existence, and came into the limelight through his clever handling of the Bravo case. Later, it became customary for the fashionable world to appeal to him in their social slips, wives who wanted divorces, husbands who did not, people who had compromised themselves in one way or another, all flocked to his little office parlour in Ely Place, where, often over a cup of tea, he gave them shrewd advice, helped them over stiles, suppressed scandal, mediated between and calmed down many ruffled couples, and made a name for himself as the lawyer who could do anything for anybody.

Small wonder he became the favourite lawyer of the Marlborough House Set!

Lewis always considered his most important case was the part he played in the acquittal of Irish Home Rule activist Charles Stewart Parnell when he unearthed the lie that had led to an accusation in *The Times*.

Throughout his life he was concerned with two other aspects of law he thought grossly unfair in respect to women. The first of these was the inequality suffered by women in respect of retaining their own property as of right on marriage and secondly the way in which the law on divorce discriminated savagely against women. This he considered cruel and socially divisive. Giving evidence before the Royal Commission on the Law of Divorce in 1910, Lewis said ladies *had told him again and again that it was torture for them to remain with the man they had married.*[16] He suggested a two year period of separation as ground for divorce.

Throughout his working life George Lewis fearlessly championed the under-dog from the customers of the Overend Gurney bank to acting for George Archer-Slee, on which case Terence Rattigan's play *The Winslow Boy* is based.

During the course of his life George Lewis became the confidant and then the friend of Edward, Prince of Wales, later King Edward VII. As the century wore on, the Prince of Wales's love of the turf, gambling and pretty women, led him into a number of difficult and embarrassing situations. He came to reply more and more upon the advice, discretion and tact of George Lewis, who became both his legal adviser and personal friend. Lewis successfully steered a middle course between the responsibility of the one and the privilege of the other. On more than one occasion Lewis had to warn the Prince against acting above the law and that his powers were limited by a parliamentary democracy — advice which the Prince found irksome, but upon which he always acted. In 1893 George Lewis was knighted. In the King Edward VII Coronation Honours list Sir George Lewis was created a baronet. He often went with the King to take the waters at Homburg, Baden or Marienbad, renting a villa, as did the king.

Sir George Lewis died on 7th December, 1911, at his home in Portland Place, London. His career ended in 1909 when he retired. As his friend King Edward VII commented, *George Lewis is the one man in England who ought to write his memories, and of course he never can*. On his retirement he took most of his confidential papers to Danish Pavilion, Pauls Lane, Overstrand where they were burned in the grounds.

Sea Marge

The German Jewish financier Edgar Speyer, and his wife, Leonora, followed their friends Sir George and Lady Lewis to Overstrand. Edgar Speyer was a member of the German Jewish family of bankers who originated from Frankfurt am Main. Descendants expanded the business to form international finance houses in London, Germany and America, where Speyer was born. He became a British subject in 1892. He was chairman of Speyer Brothers in London and a partner in the German and American branches.

Around the turn of the century Edgar Speyer met the celebrated young American violinist Leonora van Stosch. She was a woman of remarkable beauty, character and talent. She had studied music at Brussels, Paris and Leipzig and made her London debut at the first night of the proms in 1900. Edgar and Leonora were married in Germany in 1902.

About 1902 Edgar Speyer purchased the house that had once been occupied by John Morley, known as The Gables. Over the next few years on the adjoining site *regardless of cost, he erected from the finest authentic Elizabethan oak, brick and tile, a splendid house designed by the late Sir Arthur Blomfield, R.I.B.A.*, known today as Sea Marge. Blomfield is not remembered today as a domestic architect, but mainly as an ecclesiastical architect designing many churches. He designed the Royal College of Music in 1882. It seems probable he was chosen by Edgar Speyer for his knowledge of acoustics. Building work extended over a number of years. The work of enlarging the property is thought to have started in 1908. It was, however, interrupted by a fire in 1911 and was not completed until 1912. Four more gables were added to the north elevation, transforming the appearance of the house. One of the most remarkable features of the interior is the great vaulted hall with a minstrels' gallery made of wood carving believed to be Italian fifteenth century and dominated by a glorious stone mantelpiece of the same early period. It could be used is a ball room or music room.

In 1900 London was the largest city in the world and the world's financial capital. However, the transport system was piecemeal, nor was it integrated to suit the capital's needs. Trams were horse-drawn and underground trains were largely steam powered. It was at this point that the American entrepreneur Charles Yerkes arrived in London. Yerkes had transformed Chicago's transport system and is so doing had made a personal fortune. Using his vast experience of electric power, he set about achieving the same result in London. In 1901 he bought the District Line and set about electrifying it. He then turned his attention to three more underground lines in financial difficulties. The first of these was the line between Baker Street and Waterloo, known today as the Bakerloo line. This was followed by part of the present Northern line. The third was the central part of today's Piccadilly line.

By this time Yerkes was in need of financial backing. Early in 1902 he met Edgar Speyer and shared his ideas him. In Speyer he found a ready listener. In 1902 he formed an international consortium that became known as the Underground Electric Railways Consortium of London, or UERL'. Speyer Bros. and Speyer & Co. were its main backers. Edgar and ames his brother were its chief directors and Yerkes was its chairman. The aim of the 'UERL' was to finance and oversee the electrification of the Metropolitan and District lines and the construction of major sections of Bakerloo, Northern and Piccadilly lines.

Yerkes died at the end of 1905. Sir Edgar Speyer became Chairman of UERL. Speyer further tightened his grip on the London Underground in 1912 when the company purchased the Central Line and the southern section of the Northern. In the same year the *Daily Mirror* proclaimed Speyer London's 'King of the Underground'.

The Henry Wood Promenade Concerts had been launched in 1895 by Robert Newman, founder manager of the Queen's Hall Orchestra, under its conductor, Henry Wood. A few months after the marriage of Edgar and Leonora, Robert Newman went bankrupt. In order to please his wife, Edgar Speyer came to the rescue, forestalling the possibility of the orchestra being taken over by a publisher and losing autonomy. *He formed a small syndicate to take over the whole organization, Newman retaining the management of the Queen's Hall.*[17] The promenade concerts survived thanks to the foresight and generosity of Sir Edgar Speyer.

In the great music room of their luxurious home of 46, Grosvenor Street, Mayfair, presided over by John Singer Sargent's portrait of Leonora, the couple entertained some of the leading musicians and composers of the day and held musical evenings. Among those they entertained were Edvard and Mrs. Grieg, Claude Debussy, Sir Edward Elgar, Richard Strauss and Percy Grainger. Sir Edgar Speyer did much to encourage the wider appreciation of classical music in England by increasing the orchestra's professionalism, its repertoire and by making music available to a wider public as possible. Sir Henry Wood paid this tribute to him:

> The great thing was to keep up the standard of the concerts, and it was here that I found Speyer a true friend. Both he and his wife took a deep interest in everything we produced. Speyer himself was most generous in the cause of good music. However many rehearsals I asked for in order to ensure a perfect performance of a work, he agreed without a murmur.[18]

When Speyer finally left England, *he left it richer in music than he found it — at a cost of over £30,000 to himself*. Musical evenings were also hosted in the imposing music room, with its high ceiling and minstrels' gallery, that Edgar and Leonora built at Sea Marge, Overstrand.

Besides music, Speyer was involved in many other philanthropic activities and charities. As a founder trustee, he financed the Whitechapel Art Gallery. At one time he undertook voluntary work in Toynbee Hall, in the East End of London. He was President of the Poplar Hospital, taking an active concern in the welfare of the patients. Without Edgar Speyer's generous sponsoring, neither of Captain Scott's two Antarctic expeditions could have taken place. A letter to Sir Edgar was found on Scott's body containing the words, *I thank you a thousand times for your help and support and your generous kindness.*

Edgar Speyer was equally at home was in the heart of the British establishment. When the Liberals, under Henry Campbell-Bannerman, swept into power in the 1906 general election, Lord Revelstoke, head of Barings Bank, gave a dinner party to introduce Asquith to senior officials of the Bank of England and leading financiers. Among those present was Edgar Speyer.[19] He was created a Baronet in 1906, and made a member of the Privy Council in 1909.

During his association with Overstrand, Sir Edgar Speyer was well liked and bestowed his generosity on the village. On New Year's Day, 1912, he gave a *splendid treat*. The school room was converted into a miniature theatre with a proscenium arch. A troupe of Messrs Ashton's celebrated

Sea Marge, from the cliff top.

C.D.K. Minstrels was brought down from London. A Christmas tree was provided with presents for all. There were two performances: one in the afternoon for the children and another in the evening for the adults. Among the audience that evening was Lady Elizabeth Lewis, widow of Sir George Lewis.

With the outbreak of the war with Germany in 1914, his fortunes changed dramatically. He had a German name and his wife had a German name, although both were born in America. As an irrational and xenophobic German antipathy swept the nation. Sir Edgar and Lady Leonora were accused of being pro-German. Wild rumours spread that lights had been flashing from their home, Sea Marge in Overstrand, on the edge of the North Sea – the German Ocean – and that they were spies. The Chief Constable of Norfolk requested permission from the Home Secretary to search the premises, considered necessary as Sir Edgar was a Privy Counsellor. The enquiry was passed to the recently formed counter-intelligence department known as MI5. *Captain Vernon Kell replied that his organisation had 'gone into the issue very thoroughly'. As far as Sir Edgar was concerned, Kell had it 'on very high authority he is quite all right'.*[20] Anti-German propaganda and fear of spies grew worse as the war prolonged and it was plain there would be no early ending.

The full story of the appalling treatment meted out by the British government and many of their former friends to Sir Edgar and Lady Speyer is beyond the scope of this book.[21] Sir Edgar and Lady Speyer sailed to America in the spring of 1915. There is no happy ending to the story. In 1921 Sir Edgar was stripped of British citizenship under the British Nationality and Status Aliens Act. He was also stripped of his Baronetcy and membership of the Privy Council. He died in 1932, aged 69.

It has been written:

While Edgar's public benefactions were legion, so too was his private generosity, which he made no boast of, being one of those who, it is no affection to say — Do good by stealth, and blush to find it fame.

Edgar Speyer has been described as a Colossus. His drive, enthusiasm, imagination, wide range of interests, generosity and benevolence, quite apart from his achievements, are astounding. He was one of the greatest of men to be associated with Poppy land.

1   Constance Battersea, *Reminiscences* (London: Macmillan, 1922), p. 373.
2   Corner Cottage or House acquired its present name of Danum House more recently. The owner told the author it was so named because he was bnorn in Doncaster, of which Danum is the Roman name. It has no connection to Danish House Gardens or the Danish Pavilion.
3   Mary Richardson, *The Life of a Great Sportsman: John Maunsell Richardson* (London: Vinton & Co., 1919), p. 42.
4   Edward Chandos Leigh, *Bar, Bat and Bit: recollections & experiences* (London: John Murray, 1913), p. 151.
5   Richardson, p. 95.
6   Richardson, p. 174.
7   Richardson, p. 200.
8   Chautuaqua: a literary or religious convention held in a central meeting hall/tent, surrounded by tents of the participants.
9   Jane Ridley, *The Heir Apparent* (London: Chatto & Windus, 2012; Random House, 2013), p. 85.
10   Augustine Birrell, *Frederick Locker-Lampson: a character sketch* (London: Constable, 1920), pp. 78-79.
11   Frederick Locker-Lampson, *My Confidences: an autobiographical sketch addressed to my descendants* ed. Augustine Birrell (London: Smith, Elder, 1896).
12   Birrell, p. 100.
13   Birrell, p. 140.
14   C.C. Hoyer Millar, *George du Maurier and Others* (London: Cassell, 1937), p. 60.
15   John Juxon, *Lewis and Lewis* (London: Collins, 1983), p. 61.
16   Juxon, p. 301.
17   Henry J. Wood, *My Life in Music* (London: Victor Gollancz, 1938), pp. 156-157.
18   Wood, p. 157.
19   Philip Ziegler, *The Sixth Great Power: Barings 1762-1929* (London: Collins, 1988), p. 278.
20   Antony Lentin, *Banker, Traitor, Scapegoat, Spy?: the troublesome case of Sir Edgar Speyer: an episode of the Great War* (London: Haus Publishing, 2013), p. 46.
21   For a full account of this see Lentin.

Bibliography

Norfolk Record Office:

NRO GTN 3/1/14/8
NRO. GTN 3/2/1/2
NRO. GTN 3/2/1/3
NRO GTN 3/4/6/3
NRO GTN 350/106/711X2

Cromer Museum:

CRRMU 80.52.1
CRRMU 1981.80.1678
Overstrand *The Village of Millionaires', A Study of Architectural Development, 1888-1914;*
    University of St. Andrews, Dept. of Art History, Senior Honours Dissertation, 1993,
    Frances Flower.
Cromer Preservation Society Guides
No. 2: An Esplanady Sort of Place
No. 3: Pretty Villas & Capacious Hotels
No. 5: Holiday Queen Anne

Cromer Preservation Society Guides

No. 2: An Esplanady Sort of Place
No. 3: Pretty Villas & Capacious Hotels
No. 5: Holiday Queen Anne

General

Abdy, Jane, & Charlotte Gere, *The Souls* (London: Sidgwick & Jackson, 1984).
Alec-Tweedie, Ethel, *My Table-cloths: a few reminiscences* (New York: George H. Doran
    Company, 1916).
Anderson, Verily, *Friends and Relations* (London: Hodder and Stoughton, 1980).
Anderson, Verily, *The Northrepps Grandchildren* (London: Hodder and Stoughton, 1968).
Asquith, Margot, *Margot Asquith's Great War Diary, 1914—1916: the view from Downing Street*
    ed. Michael and Eleanor Brock (Oxford: Oxford University Press, 2014).
Bardswell, Frances A., *Sea-Coast Gardens and Gardening* (London: Sherratt and Hughes,
    1908).
Bartell, Edmund Jnr., *Observations upon the Town of Cromer Considered as a Watering Place*
    (Holt, 1800).

Battersea, Constance, Reminiscences (London: Macmillan, 1922).

Benson, E.F., As We Were (London: Hogarth Press, 1985).

Benson, E.F., Limitations (London: Ward, Lock, 1896).

Benson, E.F., Mrs. Ames (1912).

Bidwell, W.H., Annals of an East Anglian Bank (Norwich: Agas H. Goose, 1900).

Birrell, Augustine, Frederick Locker-Lampson: a character sketch (London: Constable, 1920).

Bolt, Rodney, The Impossible Life of Mary Benson (London: Atlantic Books, 2012).

Broadhurst, Henry, Henry Broadhurst, M.P.: The story of his life from a stonemason's bench to the Treasury bench (London: Hutchinson, 1901).

Brown, Jane, Lutyens and the Edwardians: an English architect and his clients (London: Viking, 1996).

Buxton, Ellen, Ellen Buxton's Journal arranged by Ellen R.C. Creighton (London: Geoffrey Bles, 1967).

Buxton, Ellen, Family Sketchbook a Hundred Years Ago (London: Geoffrey Bles, 1964).

Canwell, Diane, and Jonathan Sutherland, Pocket Guide to Gilbert and Sullivan (Barnsley: Remember When, 2011).

Carnie, T. West, In Quaint East Anglia (Greening, 1899).

Churchill, Winston, and Clementine Churchill, Speaking for Themselves: the personal letters of Winston and Clementine Churchill ed. Mary Soames (London: Doubleday, 1998; Black Swan, 1999).

Cooper, John, The Unexpected Story of Nathaniel Rothschild (London: Bloomsbury, 2015).

Cox, Peter, The Divided Village (Sheringham: Courtyard Publishing, 2000).

Cox, Peter, The Village Becomes a Town (Sheringham: Courtyard Publishing, 2001).

Cust, Lionel, King Edward VII and His Court (London: John Murray, 1930).

Davenport-Hines, Richard, Ettie: the intimate life and dauntless spirit of Lady Desborough (London: Weidenfeld and Nicolson, 2008).

De Courcy, Anne, The Viceroy's Daughters: the lives of the Curzon sisters (London: Weidenfeld and Nicolson, 2000).

Du Maurier, George, The Young George du Maurier: a selection of his letters, 1860—67 ed. Daphne Du Maurier (London: Peter Davies, 1951).

Farjeon, Eleanor, A Nursery in the Nineties (London: Victor Gollancz, 1935; Oxford: Oxford University Press, 1980).

Feltham, John, A Guide to all the Watering and Sea Bathing Places (London: Longman, Hurst, Rees, Orme and Brown, 1813).

Friedman, David M., Wilde in America (New York: W.W. Norton, 2014).

Hamilton, Walter, The Aesthetic Movement in England (London: Reeves & Turner, 1882; 3rd ed. reprinted by Pumpernickel Press, 2011)

Hare, Augustus J.C., The Gurneys of Earlham (London: George Allen, 1895), 3 vols.

F.G. Heath, Illustrations (W.S. Kent & Co., 1888).

Hemingway, Andrew, The Norwich School of Painters, 1803—1833 (Oxford: Phaidon, 1979).

Hilton, H.F., The Eastern Union Railway, 1846—1862 (L.N.E.R., 1946).

Holden, C. Crawford, The Tragic Empress (Unpublished typescript in Norwich Millennium library)

Holmes, David, The How Hill Story (Ludham: How Hill Trust, 1988).

Joby, R.S., The East Norfolk Railway (Norwich: Klofron, 1975).

Jolliffe, John, Raymond Asquith: life and letters (London: Collins, 1980).

Jones, Elizabeth, Poppyland in Pictures (Cromer: Poppyland Publishing, 1983).

Juxon, John, Lewis and Lewis (London: Collins, 1983).

Ketton-Cremer, R.W., Felbrigg: the story of a house (London: Rupert Hart-Davis, 1962).

Lambourne, Lionel, The Aesthetic Movement (London: Phaidon, 1996).

Langtry, Lillie, The Days I Knew (London: Hutchinson, 1925).

Leary, Patrick, *The Punch Brotherhood: table talk and print culture in mid-Victorian London* (London: British Library Board, 2010).

Leigh, Edward Chandos, *Bar, Bat and Bit: recollections & experiences* (London: John Murray, 1913).

Lentin, Antony, *Banker, Traitor, Scapegoat, Spy?: the troublesome case of Sir Edgar Speyer: an episode of the Great War* (London: Haus Publishing, 2013).

Locker-Lampson, Frederick, *My Confidences: an autobiographical sketch addressed to my descendants* ed. Augustine Birrell (London: Smith, Elder, 1896).

Marriott, William, *Forty Years of a Norfolk Railway: Sheringham, Midland and Great Northern* (Midland & Great Northern Joint Railway Society Publications, 1974).

Masters, Brian, *The Life of E.F. Benson* (London: Chatto and Windus, 1991; Pimlico, 1993).

Millar, C.C. Hoyer, *George du Maurier and Others* (London: Cassell, 1937).

Morley, John, *Recollections*, vol. 1 (London: Macmillan, 1917).

Mottram, Ralph, *Autobiography with a Difference* (London: Robert Hale, 1938).

Moyle, Franny, *Constance: the tragic and scandalous life of Mrs Oscar Wilde* (London: John Murray, 2011).

Munkman, Charles A., *The Catholic Revival in North Norfolk: centenary of Our Lady of Refuge Church in Cromer, 1895–1995* (Cromer: Church of Our Lady of Refuge, 1995).

New Approaches to Ruskin: thirteen essays ed. Robert Hewison (London: Routledge & Kegan Paul, 1981).

Ormond, Leonée, *George du Maurier* (London: Routledge & Kegan Paul, 1969).

Owen, Roger, *Lord Cromer: Victorian Imperialist, Edwardian Proconsul* (Oxford: Oxford University Press, 2004).

Pennell, Joseph, *Highways & Byways in East Anglia* (London: Macmillan, 1904).

Pipe, Christopher, *A Dictionary of Cromer and Overstrand History* (Cromer: Poppyland Publishing, 2010).

Rappaport, Helen, *Beautiful for ever: Madame Rachel of Bond Street: cosmetician, con-artist and blackmailer* (London: Vintage Books, 2012).

Reid, Andy (ed.), *Cromer and Sheringham: the growth of the holiday trade 1877–1914*, Creative History from East Anglian Sources No 3 (Norwich: Centre of East Anglian Studies in association with the Norfolk & Norwich Branch of the Historical Association, 1986).

Richardson, Mary, *The Life of a Great Sportsman: John Maunsell Richardson* (London: Vinton & Co., 1919).

Ridley, Jane, *The Heir Apparent: a life of Edward VII, the playboy prince* (London: Chatto & Windus, 2012; New York: Random House, 2013).

Rothschild, Louise Montefiore de, Lady, *Lady de Rothschild: extracts from her notebooks, with a preface by her daughter Constance Battersea* (London: Arthur L. Humphreys, 1912).

Rye, Walter, *Cromer Past and Present* (Norwich: Jarrold, 1889).

Savin, Alfred Collison, *Cromer in the County of Norfolk: a modern history* (Holt: Rounce & Wortley, 1937).

Scott, Clement, *The Drama of Yesterday & Today* (London: Macmillan, 1899), 2 vols.

Scott, Clement, *Lays and Lyrics* (London: George Routledge & Sons, 1888).

Scott, Clement, *Poppy-land: papers descriptive of scenery on the East Coast*, 4th ed. (London: Jarrold & Sons, 1895).

Scott, Margaret (Mrs. Clement Scott), *Old Days in Bohemian London: recollections of Clement Scott* (New York: Frederick A. Stokes Company, 1919).

Small, Ian (ed.), *The Aesthetes: a sourcebook* (London: Routledge and Kegan Paul, 1979).

Soames, Mary, *Clementine Churchill* (London: Cassell, 1979).

Stibbons, Peter, and David Cleveland, *Poppyland: strands of Norfolk history* (Cromer: Poppyland Publishing, 2001).

Stibbons, Frederick, *In the King's Country* (London: Henry Hartley, 1930).
Suffield, Charles Harbord, 5th Baron Suffield, *My Memories, 1830–1913* (London: Herbert Jenkins, 1913).
Tennyson, Emily Sellwood, Lady, *Lady Tennyson's Journal* ed. James O. Hoge (Charlottesville, VA: University Press of Virginia, 1981).
Tinniswood, Adrian, *The Long Weekend: life in the English country house between the wars* (London: Jonathan Cape, 2016).
Walker, Jonathan, *The Blue Beast: power & passion in the Great War* (Stroud: History Press, 2012).
Warren, Martin, *Around Cromer* (Stroud: Alan Sutton, 1995).
Watts-Dunton, Clara, *The Home Life of Swinburne* (London: A.M. Philpot, 1922).
Webb, Beatrice, *The Diary of Beatrice Webb* ed. Norman and Jeanne MacKenzie, vol. 3 (London: Virago, 1984).
Wood, Henry J., *My Life in Music* (London: Victor Gollancz, 1938).
Ziegler, Philip, *The Sixth Great Power: Barings 1762–1929* (London: Collins, 1988).

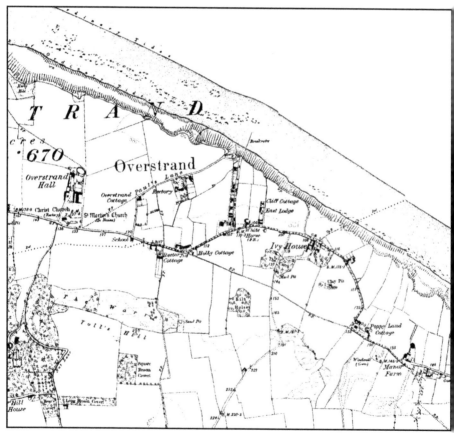

Poppyland as Clement Scott knew it in the 1888 OS map. Sidestrand mill is bottom right; Mill House is already known as Poppyland Cottage. The lane down which Scott would have walked (page 39) is top left.

Index

Lightning Source UK Ltd.
Milton Keynes UK
UKHW02f1954290318
320233UK00005B/39/P

9 781909 796348